Bob Mackin

RECORD-BREAKING
BASEBALL
TRIVIA

GREYSTONE BOOK

Douglas & McIntyre Publishing Grou
Vancouver/Toronto/New York

For Dorothy Dingwall and George Patterson

Greystone Books
A division of Douglas & McIntyre Ltd.
2323 Quebec Street, Suite 201
Vancouver, British Columbia V5T 4S7

Canadian Cataloguing in Publication Data
Mackin, Bob, 1970–
    Record-breaking baseball trivia
    ISBN 1-55054-757-7
    1. Baseball—Miscellanea. I. Title.
GV867.3.M32 2000   796.357   C00-910147-0

Editing by John Eerkes
Cover design by Peter Cocking
Front cover photograph courtesy Ron Vesely
Typeset by Tanya Lloyd/Spotlight Designs
Printed and bound in Canada by Transcontinental Printing
Printed on acid-free paper

We gratefully acknowledge the financial support of the Canada Council for the Arts, the British Columbia Ministry of Tourism, Small Business and Culture, and the Government of Canada through the Book Publishing Industry Development Program (BPIDP) for our publishing activities.

CONTENTS

INTRODUCTION

Baseball is a game of names and numbers. Its many keen observers are inspired to pay close attention to the extremes. The highest and lowest. Best and worst. Most and least. Biggest and smallest. The records.

Records are how baseball is measured from day to day and from generation to generation. But baseball's rules, regulations and playing conditions have not been the same from day one – whenever and wherever that was.

In 1887, National League batters needed five balls to walk but weren't declared out unless they got four strikes. Until 1947, a whole race of players – African-Americans – wasn't allowed to play in the two leagues that claimed to offer the sport's biggest, most prestigious stage. Until Houston's Astrodome opened in 1965, Major League baseball was only played outdoors.

Regardless, records can confirm a star's position in the lofty heights of the sport. Or they can catapult a utility player into the stratosphere.

Consider Don Larsen. The journeyman pitched 14 years but never won more or saved more than 11 games in a season. His statistics weren't worthy of induction into baseball's Hall of Fame. But what he did in one game on October 8, 1956, compensated for an unspectacular career.

Larsen's perfect game five victory for the New York Yankees in the World Series is something neither Cy Young nor Nolan Ryan nor any other pitcher managed before or since. The same can be said for Pittsburgh Pirate Harvey Haddix, who pitched a perfect 12 innings but lost 1–0 to the Milwaukee Braves in the 13th inning on May 26, 1959.

Not having lived in a city with a Major League team, I traveled to Seattle, Toronto and San Francisco for a taste of big league baseball and patiently waited for the infrequent spring training exhibitions at my hometown dome, B.C. Place Stadium. Back in the summer of 1983, I saw Major League old-timers like Hank Aaron and Roger Maris play the first baseball game under that dome.

I also witnessed players like Mark McGwire and Sammy Sosa hone their skills when they passed through the local triple A ballpark, on their way to the majors. That ballpark, Nat Bailey Stadium, was where at age eight I saw my first pro baseball game. A decade later I was working in the press box, assisting public-address announcer Pat Karl – a lifelong Cleveland Indians fan.

Over three days in 1989, I was thrilled to observe Vancouver Canadians pitcher Tom Drees and catcher Jerry Willard combine for three no-hitters in the Pacific Coast League – including two in a row on May 23 and 28: Drees and the C's beat the Calgary Cannons and Edmonton Trappers 1–0 both times. The third "no-no" came on August 16 in a 5–0 win over the Las Vegas Stars. (The second and third games were in PCL-regulation seven-inning doubleheaders.)

Drees was coached by journeyman ex–Major League pitcher Moe Drabowsky. He didn't get the call to join the parent Chicago White Sox until September 1991. Sadly, he only got the proverbial "cup of coffee" as a reliever for 7 ⅓ innings in four games.

Willard spent more time in "the show." He enjoyed six seasons with eight teams, including a stint as a pinch-hitter in the 1991 World Series for the Atlanta Braves.

But the Drees–Willard battery accomplished something Larsen and his catcher Yogi Berra didn't: three no-hitters in a season.

This book notes the achievements of DiMaggio, Ruth, Rose, Young and Cobb. But it also honors the feats of the average guys who did above-average things on a baseball diamond.

BOB MACKIN
January 2000

1

LEADING OFF

Where to begin? At the start, of course. And baseball was started at Cooperstown, New York, right? A former cow pasture in the central New York village is where Abner Doubleday supposedly invented the game one day in 1839. Many baseball historians have argued against the theory, which was accepted as fact by a United States government committee in 1907. No one, however, can dispute that Cooperstown has since 1939 been the home of the National Baseball Hall of Fame and Museum, a place where great achievements and innovations in baseball are celebrated. Regardless of where, when or who got the game going, baseball is a sport known for its athletic challenge and strategic intrigue. Here are some questions to get you started. May you be challenged and intrigued.

(Answers are on page 5.)

1.1 **What was the score of the first National League game?**
   A. 1–0
   B. 3–2
   C. 10–5
   D. 6–5

1.2 **How many times did the New York Yankees lose the World Series before winning their first championship?**
   A. Once
   B. Twice
   C. Three times
   D. Four times

1.3   **What was Babe Ruth's first Major League team?**
A. New York Yankees
B. Boston Braves
C. Boston Red Sox
D. New York Giants

1.4   **Which pitcher has the most opening-day victories?**
A. Tom Seaver
B. Juan Marichal
C. Walter Johnson
D. Nolan Ryan

1.5   **Why was Bob Feller's opening-day shutout in 1940 so extraordinary?**
A. It was his 50th victory
B. He struck out 18 batters
C. It was the first opening-day no-hitter
D. It was a perfect game

1.6   **Who was the first president of the United States of America to throw out the ceremonial first pitch on opening day?**
A. William Howard Taft
B. Dwight D. Eisenhower
C. Franklin D. Roosevelt
D. Ronald Reagan

1.7   **Who was the first recipient of the Rookie of the Year Award in 1947?**
A. Jackie Robinson
B. Larry Jansen
C. Don Newcombe
D. Joe DiMaggio

1.8 Where was the first All-Star Game played?
A. Comiskey Park, Chicago
B. Wrigley Field, Chicago
C. Yankee Stadium, New York
D. Municipal Stadium, Cleveland

1.9 Where did the Dodgers play their first home game after moving to Los Angeles in 1958?
A. Dodger Stadium
B. Los Angeles Memorial Coliseum
C. Rose Bowl
D. Los Angeles Memorial Sports Arena

1.10 What expansion team won the first Major League regular-season game in Canada?
A. Toronto Blue Jays
B. California Angels
C. Montreal Expos
D. Seattle Mariners

1.11 How many RBIs did Hank Aaron register in his first at-bat on opening day 1974 to tie Babe Ruth's all-time home run record?
A. One
B. Two
C. Three
D. Four

1.12 Where was the first regular-season Major League baseball game played under a dome?
A. Seattle
B. Houston
C. Minneapolis
D. New York

1.13   What year did the designated hitter rule come into effect in the American League?
A. 1951
B. 1969
C. 1973
D. 1984

1.14   Bob Watson was the first player to hit for the cycle in both the American League and National League. Which teams did he play for to make history?
A. Chicago White Sox and Chicago Cubs
B. New York Mets and New York Yankees
C. Houston Astros and Boston Red Sox
D. Baltimore Orioles and San Francisco Giants

1.15   Which player was the first to hit more than two home runs on opening day?
A. Karl "Tuffy" Rhodes
B. Mark McGwire
C. Sammy Sosa
D. George Bell

1.16   Which team won the first regular-season game between American League and National League teams?
A. Texas Rangers
B. Milwaukee Brewers
C. Toronto Blue Jays
D. San Francisco Giants

1.17   Where did Mark McGwire hit his first home run during his record-setting 1998 season?
A. Dodger Stadium, Los Angeles
B. Olympic Stadium, Montreal
C. Busch Stadium, St. Louis
D. Pro Player Stadium, Miami

1.18 How many teams had pitcher Mike Morgan pitched for after
19 seasons?
A. Six
B. Nine
C. 11
D. 14

1.19 Which city's team joined the National League in 1998?
A. Los Angeles
B. Chicago
C. Montreal
D. Milwaukee

LEADING OFF
Answers

1.1 **D. 6–5**
Play ball! Athletic Park in Philadelphia was the site of the first
National League game, a 6–5 Boston Red Stockings win over the
Philadelphia Athletics on April 22, 1876. The two-hour and
45-minute game was played before 3,000 fans. Boston center
fielder Jim O'Rourke had the first hit, and Joseph Borden was the
winning pitcher. The NL is the oldest continuously operating
professional sports league in the United States. It was the suc-
cessor to the National Association, which began play in 1871.
The American League wasn't established until 1901.

1.2 **B. Twice**
For the New York Yankees it was third time lucky. They lost two
consecutive World Series to the rival New York Giants before
beating the Giants four games to two in 1923's fall classic. The
teams shared the Polo Grounds stadium, where the Giants won
the 1921 and 1922 World Series. But the Yankees moved across
the Harlem River to the new Yankee Stadium in the Bronx in
1923. They met the Giants again in that year's World Series, but

the Yankees seemed more at home in their former ballpark. They won three of their four World Series games at the Polo Grounds, preventing the Giants from gaining a third consecutive crown. Babe Ruth led both teams with three home runs. The Yankees won their record 25th World Series in 1999 at Yankee Stadium.

1.3   **C.   Boston Red Sox**
George Herman "Babe" Ruth made his Major League debut on July 11, 1914, as a member of the Boston Red Sox. The Baltimore native was 2–1 on the mound and had ten at-bats in five games that year. He played for the Red Sox until 1919, when he was sold during the off-season to the rival New York Yankees for $100,000 cash and a $350,000 loan. (Red Sox owner Harry Frazee had financial difficulties, stemming from his live-theater productions.) Ruth hit a then-record 54 home runs the next season as a Yankee. The deal broke the hearts of many Red Sox fans, who continue to blame Frazee for their team's World Series drought. With Babe, the Red Sox won three World Series. In the post-Ruth era, the Red Sox have lost four World Series – all four games to three. Ruth played 15 years for the Yankees and won four World Series before returning to Boston to end his career in 1935. His swan song came with the National League's Braves.

1.4   **C.   Walter Johnson**
Washington Senators ace Walter Johnson was always rarin' and ready to go on opening day. He was 9–5 with 14 complete games and seven shutouts on opening day. "Big Train" Johnson spent his entire 21-year career with the Senators. He also managed the Senators from 1929 to 1932.

1.5   **C.   It was the first opening-day no-hitter**
On April 16, 1940, Cleveland Indians pitcher Bob Feller pitched the first opening-day no-hit victory in Major League history with a 1–0 shutout of the Chicago White Sox at Comiskey Park. It was also the first of three no-hitters Feller would register during his career. He pitched two more for the Indians in 1946 and 1951.

1.6   **A. William Howard Taft**

President William Howard Taft began a tradition when he became the first president to offer the ceremonial pitch on April 14, 1910, in Washington, D.C. Umpire Billy Evans asked the president to throw the ball over the plate before Walter Johnson pitched the Washington Senators to a 3–0 one-hit win over the Philadelphia Athletics. There was little fanfare, and Taft made one more opening-day pitch during his term of office. Franklin D. Roosevelt made the most opening-day ceremonial pitches, with eight to his credit.

DID YOU KNOW?

Chicago is the only city to continuously field a team in the National League since the league's 1876 establishment. In fact, the White Stockings were the NL's first champions in 1876, with a 52–14 record. Chicago manager/pitcher A.G. Spalding (who later became a sporting-goods manufacturer) led the league with 47 victories. In 1871, the team was among the nine founding members of the NL's predecessor, the National Association of Professional Base Ball Players. Its names included the Colts and the Orphans before the franchise was dubbed the Cubs at the turn of the century. Play in the American League got underway on April 24, 1901, when owner Charles Comiskey's Chicago White Stockings beat the Cleveland Blues 8–2 in a Chicago park normally used for cricket. The teams were later renamed the White Sox and the Indians.

1.7   **A. Jackie Robinson**

Jackie Robinson of the Brooklyn Dodgers was voted rookie of the year by 39 members of the Baseball Writers' Association of America after batting .297 and hitting 12 home runs in his first Major League season. Each voting committee member was asked to submit a list of five rookies, in order of preference. Robinson received 129 points. Larry Jansen of the New York Giants was in second place   points back. Robinson was awarded the J. Louis Comiskey Memorial Award. During the Hall of Fame induction ceremony 40 years later, the Rookie of the Year Award was renamed the Jackie Robinson Award in honor of the first African-American to play Major League baseball.

1.8   **A. Comiskey Park, Chicago**
July 6, 1933, was a star-studded day at Chicago's Comiskey Park, the site of the first Major League baseball All-Star Game. The American League, led by pitcher Lefty Gomez, defeated the National League 4–2. The New York Yankees' Gomez was the first All-Star winning pitcher and the first to register an RBI in the midsummer classic when he singled home Jimmy Dykes of the hometown Chicago White Sox in the second inning. Another Yankee, Babe Ruth, hit a two-run homer in the third inning before 49,200 fans. *Chicago Tribune* sports editor Arch Ward lobbied for the creation of the All-Star Game to complement the 1933 World's Fair in Chicago.

1.9   **B. Los Angeles Memorial Coliseum**
When Dodgers owner Walter O'Malley moved his team from Brooklyn, New York, to the west coast after the 1957 season, he chose Los Angeles Memorial Coliseum as the team's new home. The Coliseum, site of the 1932 Olympic Games, was the temporary home of the Dodgers until Dodger Stadium was built in 1962. The team opened its first season in Los Angeles on April 18, 1958, before 78,672 fans with a 6–5 win over the San Francisco Giants. Visitor Hank Sauer hit the first home run at the converted football stadium. Only 6,702 fans were at the last game in Ebbets Field on September 24, 1957. They saw the Dodgers beat the Pittsburgh Pirates 2–0.

1.10   **C. Montreal Expos**
The Expos were the first Major League franchise outside the United States and hosted the first regular-season game on foreign soil on April 14, 1969, an 8–7 win over the St. Louis Cardinals at Jarry Park in Montreal before 29,184 fans.

1.11   C. Three

"Hammerin'" Hank Aaron hit a three-run homer in the first inning on April 4, 1974, off Cincinnati Reds pitcher Jack Billingham in Cincinnati's Riverfront Stadium. Aaron swung for the first time of the season on the first pitch offered by Billingham to hit his 714th home run. The homer tied Babe Ruth's career mark. Aaron's Atlanta Braves, however, lost the game 7–6. During the Braves' home opener four days later on April 8, 1974, Aaron sent a pitch by Los Angeles Dodger Al Downing into the bleachers for his record 715th home run. It was the last time Aaron opened a season for Atlanta. He played his final two years with the Milwaukee Brewers and finished with 755 career homers.

1.12   B. Houston

On April 12, 1965, the Philadelphia Phillies spoiled the Houston Astros' regular season debut at their new home in a dome. The Phillies were 2–0 winners of Major League baseball's first game in the 54,370-seat Harris County Domed Stadium. Later renamed the Astrodome, the $31.7 million facility hosted its first baseball game three days earlier, on April 9, 1965. The Astros beat the New York Yankees 2–1 in a 12-inning exhibition game. Yankee Mickey Mantle had the first home run before 47,878 fans. The first dome in baseball originally had a natural grass field and 4,796 clear panes of glass in its roof, but the glare prevented some fielders from seeing the ball. Part of the roof was painted, but the grass died. The solution? Artificial turf, dubbed Astroturf, was installed midway through the 1966 season. The Astros vacated the Astrodome in 1999 after losing a National League divisional series to the Atlanta Braves. Their new home in 2000 was retractable-roofed Enron Field.

1.13   C. 1973

On April 6, 1973, New York Yankee Ron Blomberg became the first official designated hitter when he came to bat against Boston Red Sox pitcher Luis Tiant in Boston's Fenway Park. Blomberg walked with the bases loaded and finished one-for-three in the Yankees' 15–5 opening-day loss. The American League voted unanimously for the rule change in time for the 1973 season, but the National League resisted the controversial innovation. The DH rule allows a non-fielding player to substitute for the pitcher in the batting order at the start of the game. It gave managers a chance to bolster their offence while preserving the pitcher for his mound duties. The NL never adopted the DH rule, but its teams use a DH when they visit AL parks. Conversely, AL teams can't use the DH when they travel to NL parks.

1.14   C.   Houston Astros and Boston Red Sox
Bob Watson is baseball's only interleague "cyclist." As a member of the Houston Astros, he singled, doubled, tripled and hit a home run June 24, 1977, in a game against the San Francisco Giants. He repeated the feat, but with the Boston Red Sox in the American League on September 15, 1979, in a 10–2 win over the Baltimore Orioles.

1.15   D.   George Bell
George Bell rang in the 1988 season in style on April 4. He was the first batter to hit three home runs on opening day when his Toronto Blue Jays beat the Kansas City Royals 5–3 in Kansas City. Karl "Tuffy" Rhodes of the Chicago Cubs joined Bell in the record books on April 8, 1994, when he had three homers in the Cubs' 12–8 loss to the New York Mets.

1.16   D.   San Francisco Giants
The National League's San Francisco Giants beat the American League's Texas Rangers 4–3 on June 12, 1997, at the Ballpark in Arlington, Texas, to end the traditional regular-season isolation of the two major leagues. Interleague play brought fans back to the ballparks in droves.

1.17   **C. Busch Stadium, St. Louis**
Mark McGwire had 58 home runs in 1997 – 34 with Oakland and 24 with St. Louis. He renewed the conquest of Roger Maris's single-season home run record with a grand slam at Busch Stadium in St. Louis on March 31, 1998. Los Angeles Dodgers pitcher Ramon Martinez surrendered the bases-loaded homer as the Cardinals eventually won the opening-day game 6–0. McGuire ended the year on September 27, also at Busch Stadium, with home run number 70.

1.18   **C. 11**
Right-handed pitcher Mike Morgan joined the Texas Rangers – his record 11th Major League team – on April 7, 1999. He debuted in the Major Leagues in 1978, with the Oakland Athletics, and after that saw action with the New York Yankees, Toronto Blue Jays, Seattle Mariners, Baltimore Orioles, Los Angeles Dodgers, Chicago Cubs, St. Louis Cardinals, Cincinnati Reds and Minnesota Twins.

1.19   **D. Milwaukee**
The Milwaukee Brewers were the first American League team to change leagues. The Brewers moved to the National League to even the membership ranks at 16 after the introduction of the expansion Arizona Diamondbacks. In the Brewers' first NL game on March 31, 1998, they lost 2–1 to the Braves in Atlanta. The Braves, incidentally, moved from Milwaukee to their current home in 1966. The Brewers began play in Milwaukee in 1970, after the American League's Seattle Pilots moved to the Wisconsin city.

Game One

RECORD NUMBERS

Match the names of the players with the record numbers that made them famous.

(*Answers are on page 120.*)

1. _____ Cal Ripken Jr.   A. 4,256 career hits

2. _____ Mark McGwire   B. 59 consecutive scoreless innings pitched

3. _____ Hank Aaron   C. 511 career pitching wins

4. _____ Pete Rose   D. 56 consecutive games with a hit

5. _____ Joe DiMaggio   E. 191 RBIs in a season

6. _____ Nolan Ryan   F. 2,246 career runs scored

7. _____ Hack Wilson   G. 755 career home runs

8. _____ Orel Hershiser   H. 5,714 career strikeouts pitched

9. _____ Connie Mack   I. 23 career grand slams

10. _____ Ty Cobb   J. 70 home runs in a season

11. _____ Lou Gehrig   K. 53 seasons managed

12. _____ Cy Young   L. 2,632 consecutive games

2

ROOKIES

Hope springs eternal. In baseball, hope arrives every spring with fresh new faces at training camp. The youthful players' eager presence helps breathe new life into an old game. The rookies begin their quest to gain experience, get their own spot in the batting order (and in the field) and maybe win a pennant — or, better yet, a World Series ring. This chapter explores some of the wonderful feats achieved by those who made an early mark in their Major League baseball careers. Right off the bat, as they say.

(Answers are on page 17.)

2.1   What was Joe Nuxhall's age when he became the youngest player in Major League history?
A. 13
B. 15
C. 16
D. 19

2.2   How many Houston Astros did rookie pitcher Kerry Wood strike out to set a National League record on May 6, 1998?
A. 14
B. 17
C. 20
D. 22

2.3   Who was the American League runner-up in RBIs when Ted Williams set a Major League rookie record in 1939?
A. Babe Ruth
B. Joe DiMaggio
C. Frank McCormick
D. Hank Greenberg

2.4 Who holds the Major League record for most home runs by a rookie in a season?
  A. Ken Griffey Jr.
  B. Sammy Sosa
  C. Mark McGwire
  D. Roger Maris

2.5 Who was the only rookie to bat over .400?
  A. Ted Williams
  B. Mark McGwire
  C. Joe Jackson
  D. Hank Aaron

2.6 When Tim Raines set the rookie record for most stolen bases in 1981, how many games did he play?
  A. 162
  B. 81
  C. 88
  D. 120

2.7 In 1929, rookie Johnny Frederick hit more doubles than which future Hall of Fame second baseman?
  A. Rogers Hornsby
  B. Tony Lazzeri
  C. Frankie Frisch
  D. Jackie Robinson

2.8 Benito Santiago's rookie record hitting streak lasted for how many games?
  A. 26
  B. 34
  C. 37
  D. 56

2.9 For what team did pitcher Grover Cleveland Alexander win 28 games in his 1911 rookie season?
  A. Brooklyn Dodgers
  B. Chicago White Sox
  C. St. Louis Cardinals
  D. Philadelphia Phillies

2.10 How many complete game victories did rookie Charles "Babe" Adams pitch in the 1909 World Series?
  A. None
  B. Three
  C. Four
  D. Six

2.11 Which Pittsburgh Pirate set the record for most rookie hits in 1927?
  A. Paul Waner
  B. Lloyd Waner
  C. Pie Traynor
  D. Frankie Frisch

2.12 Who was the first rookie of the year also chosen as most valuable player?
  A. Fred Lynn
  B. Reggie Jackson
  C. Johnny Bench
  D. Mark McGwire

2.13 What was Satchel Paige's age when he became the oldest rookie in Major League history?
  A. 32
  B. 37
  C. 41
  D. 42

2.14 Which team has the record for most consecutive rookie of the year winners?
A. New York Yankees
B. Brooklyn Dodgers
C. Los Angeles Dodgers
D. Boston Red Sox

2.15 Who was the first player selected in Major League baseball's first annual amateur free-agent draft in 1965?
A. Reggie Jackson
B. Les Rohr
C. Joe Coleman
D. Rick Monday

2.16 Fred Lindstrom was the youngest player in a World Series when he played third base for which team in 1924?
A. New York Giants
B. New York Yankees
C. Washington Senators
D. Detroit Tigers

2.17 What was Ty Cobb's first career hit?
A. Single
B. Double
C. Triple
D. Home run

2.18 How many players have hit a grand slam in their first Major League at-bat?
A. One
B. Two
C. Four
D. Ten

2.19 **Who was the youngest manager of all time?**
A. Sparky Anderson
B. Roger Peckinpaugh
C. Lou Boudreau
D. John McGraw

ROOKIES
Answers

2.1 **B. 15**
Joe Nuxhall was 15 years, 10 months and 11 days old when he pitched two thirds of an inning for the Cincinnati Reds on June 10, 1944. He allowed two hits and five walks in an 18–0 St. Louis Cardinals win. Nuxhall was a six-foot-three, left-handed junior high school student when he signed a contract at the start of the season with Cincinnati. After his inauspicious debut, he wasn't seen again in the majors until 1952. He finished a 16-season career in 1966 with the Reds.

2.2 **C. 20**
Chicago Cubs pitcher Kerry Wood struck out 20 Houston Astros batters in only his fifth Major League start. The Irving, Texas, native was more than a month shy of his 22nd birthday when he set the National League record for most strikeouts in a game and by a rookie. The right-handed pitcher held the Astros to one hit and allowed no walks in the game at Wrigley Field. Wood followed in his next start with 13 strikeouts in a seven-inning performance against the Arizona Diamondbacks. He completed his freshman campaign with a 13–6 record and 3.40 ERA.

2.3 **B. Joe DiMaggio**
New York Yankees center fielder Joe DiMaggio had 126 RBIs in 1939, 19 fewer than Boston Red Sox rookie Ted Williams, who had 145 in his rookie season and led the Major Leagues. Frank McCormick, however, had 128 for the Cincinnati Reds to lead the National League. Williams, a San Diego native, spent

19 years with Boston. His best year for RBIs was 1949, when he had 159.

2.4 C. Mark McGwire
First baseman Mark McGwire bashed 49 home runs in 1987 for the Oakland Athletics to win the American League home run title and rookie of the year award that season. He tied with the Chicago Cubs' Andre Dawson for the Major League lead.

2.5 C. Joe Jackson
"Shoeless" Joe Jackson of the 1911 Cleveland Naps (the Indians' name at that time) had a .408 batting average in his rookie season. The 22-year-old outfielder was second only to Detroit Tiger Ty Cobb, who hit .420. Jackson actually made his Major League debut in 1908 with the Philadelphia Athletics, but he played only five games that year and the next. He joined the Indians in 1910 but saw action in only 20 games. He was traded to the Chicago White Sox in 1915 and was part of the infamous "Black Sox" scandal of 1919. Jackson and seven teammates were banned from baseball for life after Kenesaw Mountain Landis, baseball's commissioner, found that they had conspired with gamblers to lose the World Series to the Cincinnati Reds.

2.6 C. 88
Tim Raines played just 88 games in his rookie season for the Montreal Expos when he led the majors with 71 stolen bases. Raines was caught stealing only 11 times. His nearest rival was the Oakland Athletics' base-stealing specialist, Rickey Henderson, who stole 56 in 108 games.

2.7 A. Rogers Hornsby
Chicago Cub Rogers Hornsby had five fewer doubles in 1929 than did rookie Johnny Frederick of the Brooklyn Robins (also known as the Dodgers), who led the Major Leagues with 52 doubles. Hornsby, considered by some experts the best second

baseman of all time, played 23 seasons and was elected to the Hall of Fame in 1942.

2.8 **B. 34**
In his 1987 rookie season, San Diego Padres catcher Benito Santiago hit successfully in 34 consecutive games. Los Angeles Dodgers pitcher Orel Hershiser stopped the streak on October 3, but Santiago was named the National League's rookie of the year.

2.9 **D. Philadelphia Phillies**
Grover Cleveland Alexander won a rookie record 28 games in 1911 for the Philadelphia Phillies. Alexander began his 20-season career with a 28–13 record. He led the National League by completing 31 of the 37 games he started, pitching 367 innings and shutting out seven opponents. He had four one-hitters in 1915, but his best year was 1916, when he registered 16 shutouts on the way to a 33–12 finish.

2.10 **B. Three**
The Pittsburgh Pirates' right-handed pitcher, Charles "Babe" Adams, had three complete game wins in the 1909 World Series

---

DID YOU KNOW?

The triple A International League began desegregation a year before Major League baseball did. On October 23, 1945, the Brooklyn Dodgers' general manager Branch Rickey signed Jackie Robinson to play with the Montreal Royals, Brooklyn's affiliate in the IL. In his first game, on April 18, 1946, Robinson had a home run and three singles at Roosevelt Stadium in Jersey City, New Jersey, against the Giants. He batted .349 and led the Royals to the Junior World Series championship. Robinson's Major League debut, on April 15, 1947, was less impressive. The first baseman and first African-American player in the Major Leagues was held hitless in a 5–3 Dodgers win over the Boston Braves at Ebbets Field. He batted .297 and was named the first rookie of the year.

as a rookie, leading Pittsburgh to its first championship. Adams began the series against the Detroit Tigers with a 4–1 win on October 8, had an 8–4 win five days later on October 13 and completed the series with an 8–0 game seven win on October 16. Adams, a 27-year-old rookie, had a 12–3 regular-season record and a 1.11 ERA.

2.11 **B. Lloyd Waner**
Center fielder Lloyd Waner had a rookie record 223 hits in 1927 as a 21-year-old member of the Pittsburgh Pirates. Waner's brother and teammate, 24-year-old sophomore right fielder Paul Waner, led the Major Leagues with 237 and was the National League's most valuable player. In their first year together the Harrah, Oklahoma, brothers went to the World Series, but the Pirates were swept in four games by the New York Yankees. They played together until Paul Waner was released after the 1940 season.

2.12 **A. Fred Lynn**
In 1975, Fred Lynn of the Boston Red Sox was the first rookie of the year to also be named most valuable player. The 23-year-old center fielder contributed to the Red Sox's pennant-winning season with a .331 batting average, 21 home runs and 105 RBIs. His 103 runs led the American League while he was tied with the Cincinnati Reds' Pete Rose for most Major League doubles at 47. During his 17-season career, the Chicago native also played for the California Angels, Baltimore Orioles, Detroit Tigers and San Diego Padres.

2.13 **D. 42**
Satchel Paige was signed by the Cleveland Indians in 1948, at age 42. Paige had been a star in the Negro National League beginning in the mid-1920s but had to overcome racism to become a Major League pitcher. The Indians' owner, Bill Veeck, signed Paige a year after Jackie Robinson became the first African-American to play Major League baseball. Paige started his first

game on August 3, 1948, as the Indians beat the Washington Senators 5–3. He ended his rookie season with a 6–1 record as the Indians won the American League pennant. Paige pitched two thirds of an inning as the third of four relievers in game five of the World Series against the Boston Braves. On September 25, 1965, 59-year-old Paige became the oldest Major Leaguer in history. He emerged from retirement to pitch three innings in a Kansas City Athletics loss to the Boston Red Sox.

2.14 **C. Los Angeles Dodgers**
For five consecutive years, a Los Angeles Dodger finished first in National League rookie of the year voting. The streak is the longest in both major leagues. The five award-winning rookies were first baseman Eric Karros (1992), catcher Mike Piazza (1993), right fielder Raul Mondesi (1994), pitcher Hideo Nomo (1995) and left fielder Todd Hollandsworth (1996). The Dodgers also had four NL rookies of the year from 1979 to 1982: pitchers Rick Sutcliffe, Steve Howe and Fernando Valenzuela and second baseman Steve Sax.

2.15 **D. Rick Monday**
It was a Tuesday when outfielder Rick Monday became the first player chosen in Major League baseball's inaugural amateur free-agent draft on June 8, 1965, in New York City. Monday was selected first overall by the Kansas City Athletics and signed with the team for $104,000. The 19-year-old sophomore from Arizona State University joined the Athletics in 1966 and had a 19-year career. One of his finest moments came October 19, 1981, when he hit the winning home run for the Los Angeles Dodgers in the fifth and deciding game of the National League championship series against the Montreal Expos. Monday and the Dodgers eventually beat Reggie Jackson and the New York Yankees in six games to win the World Series. Jackson was a teammate of Monday's at Arizona State and the A's first-round pick (second overall) in the 1966 draft.

2.16 **A. New York Giants**

Fred Lindstrom was the New York Giants' third baseman in the seven-game World Series loss to the Washington Senators. Lindstrom was 18 years, 10 months and 13 days old when the series began October 4, 1924. He had four hits in game five, but the seventh and deciding game was a nightmare. Senators catcher Muddy Ruel had the championship-winning run after Earl McNeely hit a ball that bounced over Lindstrom's head in the bottom of the 12th inning. Lindstrom played another 12 seasons, in seven of which he batted better than .300.

2.17 **B. Double**

At 18 years of age, Detroit Tigers rookie Ty Cobb doubled in his first Major League game on August 30, 1905, against pitcher Jack Chesbro and the New York Highlanders (the Yankees' original name). It was the first of 4,189 career hits, a record that stood until 1985.

2.18 **A. One**

Philadelphia Phillies pitcher Bill Duggleby was the first Major Leaguer to grand slam in his first career at-bat. In fact, he sent the first pitch offered by New York Giants pitcher Cy Seymour over the wall on April, 21, 1898.

2.19 **B. Roger Peckinpaugh**

Shortstop Roger Peckinpaugh managed the New York Yankees for 20 games in the 1914 season. Peckinpaugh was 23 years and seven months old when he took over from Frank Chance on September 16, 1914. He had a 10–10 record as the Yankees moved from seventh to sixth in American League standings. He resumed his career as a player the next season and didn't manage a team again until he guided the Cleveland Indians for six consecutive seasons beginning in 1928. His last year at the helm was 1941, a year before he was replaced by Lou Boudreau. Twenty-four-year-old Boudreau became the youngest person to manage a Major League team for an entire season.

Game Two

Award-Winning Rookies

Match the following baseball greats with the season and league in which they were landslide winners of the rookie of the year award.

(*Answers are on page 120.*)

1. _____ Frank Robinson (Cincinnati Reds)   A. 1997 NL

2. _____ Tony Kubek (New York Yankees)   B. 1993 AL

3. _____ Orlando Cepedo (San Francisco Giants) C. 1985 NL

4. _____ Willie McCovey (San Francisco Giants) D. 1990 AL

5. _____ Carlton Fisk (Boston Red Sox)   E. 1958 NL

6. _____ Vince Coleman (St. Louis Cardinals)   F. 1987 AL

7. _____ Mark McGwire (Oakland Athletics)   G. 1993 NL

8. _____ Benito Santiago (San Diego Padres)   H. 1987 NL

9. _____ Sandy Alomar Jr. (Cleveland Indians)   I. 1996 AL

10. _____ Tim Salmon (California Angels)   J. 1994 NL

11. _____ Mike Piazza (Los Angeles Dodgers)   K. 1972 AL

12. _____ Raul Mondesi (Los Angeles Dodgers)   L. 1957 AL

13. _____ Derek Jeter (New York Yankees)   M. 1997 AL

14. _____ Nomar Garciaparra (Boston Red Sox)   N. 1959 NL

15. _____ Scott Rolen (Philadelphia Phillies)   O. 1956 NL

3
TEAMWORK

Teams come and go. They change cities, names and uniform designs. Others stay put, create dynasties and become part of popular culture. They also become topics of longstanding disputes among baseball fans. For example, which team was baseball's greatest? Was it the 1906 Chicago Cubs, who won 116 regular-season games but only two in the World Series? Or was it the 1998 New York Yankees, who had 114 regular-season victories and another 11 in post-season to win the World Series? Whatever the answer, both teams demonstrated how individuals can effectively join forces in a singular, selfless effort as a group. Give it your best effort to answer this chapter's questions about teams.

(Answers are on page 28.)

3.1 In what city did Connie Mack, Major League baseball's longest-serving manager, begin his 53-year managerial career?
A. New York
B. Pittsburgh
C. Philadelphia
D. Chicago

3.2 How many home runs did the Toronto Blue Jays hit in a 1987 game, for the Major League record?
A. Six
B. Eight
C. Ten
D. 13

3.3 What team did the New York Giants beat to begin their Major League record winning streak in 1916?
A. New York Yankees
B. Brooklyn Robins

C. Pittsburgh Pirates

D. Chicago Cubs

3.4 **How many consecutive losses did the Cleveland Spiders record in 1899 to set the all-time Major League record?**

A. 17

B. 21

C. 23

D. 24

3.5 **The 1906 Chicago Cubs won a record 116 games. Which team spoiled the Cubs' season by beating them in the World Series?**

A. New York Giants

B. Chicago White Sox

C. Cincinnati Reds

D. Pittsburgh Pirates

3.6 **What was the home ballpark for the New York Mets when they lost a 20th-century record 120 games in 1962?**

A. Shea Stadium

B. Yankee Stadium

C. Ebbets Field

D. Polo Grounds

3.7 **The Atlanta Braves won the World Series in 1991 after finishing last place in 1990. What American League team that also finished last in 1990 did the Braves play in the fall classic?**

A. Minnesota Twins

B. Milwaukee Brewers

C. New York Yankees

D. Toronto Blue Jays

3.8 Which team had the biggest one-season turnaround in Major League history?

A. Atlanta Braves

B. Minnesota Twins

C. Chicago Cubs

D. Arizona Diamondbacks

3.9 What team won 100 regular-season games on the earliest date?

A. Cleveland Indians

B. New York Yankees

C. Arizona Diamondbacks

D. Chicago Cubs

3.10 For how many games did opponents shut out the St. Louis Cardinals in 1908?

A. Six

B. 14

C. 25

D. 33

3.11 How many innings were there in the longest tie game in Major League history?

A. 14

B. 20

C. 26

D. 29

3.12 What team was the first to retire a player's number?

A. New York Giants

B. New York Yankees

C. Pittsburgh Pirates

D. Boston Red Sox

3.13 Which American League team has moved from city to city the most without changing its name?
A. Mariners
B. Athletics
C. Dodgers
D. Braves

3.14 What is the Major League record for most runners left on base in a game?
A. 18
B. 25
C. 45
D. 50

3.15 The Chicago Cubs were the last team to begin playing night games at home. In what year did the Cubs play begin regular play under the lights at Wrigley Field for the first time?
A. 1939
B. 1987
C. 1988
D. 1999

3.16 What team won the first Major League opening-day game outside the United States or Canada?
A. Colorado Rockies
B. San Diego Padres
C. Montreal Expos
D. Florida Marlins

3.17 What is the record for most players used by both teams in a single game?
A. 23
B. 54
C. 55
D. 60

3.18 What team won the highest-scoring Major League game in history?
A. New York Yankees
B. Philadelphia Phillies
C. Los Angeles Dodgers
D. Chicago Cubs

3.19 The Seattle Mariners hit a Major League team record 264 home runs in 1997. How many were hit at home?
A. 97
B. 121
C. 129
D. 131

TEAMWORK
Answers

3.1 **B. Pittsburgh**
Connie Mack was a Major League manager for half a century, and then some. Mack, a catcher, managed the Pittsburgh Pirates from 1894 to 1896. He took over from Albert Buckenburger late in the season and helped the team to a 65–65 record. Mack spent four seasons with Milwaukee in the Western League to hone his dugout skills before returning to the Major Leagues when he was given the American League's expansion Philadelphia franchise in 1901. The team finished on top of the AL standings in its second season. Over the next 50 years, Mack's Athletics had nine AL pennants and 17 last-place finishes. More importantly, the Athletics won the World Series five times. Mack finally retired at age 88 with the most wins (3,731) and most losses (3,948) for a manager – records that may never be equaled.

3.2 **C. 10**
The Toronto Blue Jays were flying on September 14, 1987, but the Baltimore Orioles weren't. The Jays had a Major League record ten home runs in an 18–3 home win over the Orioles.

Catcher Ernie Whitt led the assault with three of his 16 1987 home runs. George Bell and Rance Mulliniks had two each, while Rob Ducey, Fred McGriff and Lloyd Moseby each contributed one.

3.3   B.   Brooklyn Robins

On September 7, 1916, the New York Giants beat their crosstown rivals, the Brooklyn Robins, 4−1 at the Polo Grounds to begin a 26-game winning streak. The Giants, managed by John McGraw, won 25 more games at home through September 30. The last day of September witnessed the Giants' first loss in more than three weeks. The Boston Braves dealt New York an 8−3 defeat in the second game of a doubleheader. That winning streak, and an earlier 17-game string of road victories, did little to help the Giants extend their season. The team finished fourth, seven games below the first-place Robins, with an 86−66 record.

3.4   D.   24

The Cleveland Spiders were stuck in a web of losses during the 1899 National League season − 24 consecutive losses, to be exact. The string of defeats began on August 26. On September 18, the Spiders edged the Washington Senators 5−4, but the celebration was brief. Cleveland embarked on a 16-game losing streak and finished in last place with just 20 wins. The Spiders' 134 losses are a Major League record.

3.5   B.   Chicago White Sox

Baseball fever engulfed Chicago when the White Sox met the Cubs for the first World Series between two teams in the same city. The White Sox won the championship in six games. The Cubs set a regular-season record for most team wins when they marked their 116th victory on October 4, 1906, with a 4−0 triumph over the Pittsburgh Pirates. They lost only 36 games during the entire season. The Cubs were led defensively by the legendary infield of shortstop Joe Tinker, second baseman Johnny Evers and first baseman Frank Chance. But it was third baseman Harry Steinfeldt who sparked the offense. Steinfeldt led the National League with 176 hits and was tied with the Pittsburgh Pirates' Jim Nealon at 83 RBIs.

3.6   **D. Polo Grounds**
The sad-sack New York Mets began their record 120-loss season at home on April 13, 1962, in the Polo Grounds. The Pittsburgh Pirates came away with a 4−3 win before 12,447 fans. The expansion Mets, managed by Casey Stengel, would win only 40 games in the ten-team National League season. The San Francisco Giants won the NL pennant with a 103−62 record.

3.7   **A. Minnesota Twins**
The Minnesota Twins were the Atlanta Braves' opposition in the 1991 World Series − the first time in modern history that two last-to-first teams met in the championship. The Twins rebounded from a 74−88 last-place finish in the American League West in 1990 with a 1991 record of 95−67. The Braves were last in the National League West in 1990 at 65−97 but were 94−68 for tops in the NL East in 1991. The Twins edged the Braves 1−0 in the tenth inning of the seventh and deciding game of the 1991 World Series on October 27.

3.8   **D. Arizona Diamondbacks**
The Arizona Diamondbacks were 65−97 in 1998, their first year of play. A year later they advanced to the National League divisional playoffs with a 100−62 tally. Arizona, a popular venue for Major League spring training, finally had a team to call its own when the Diamondbacks debuted March 31, 1998, at Bank One Ballpark in Phoenix. The Diamondbacks lost 9−2 to the Colorado Rockies at the first Major League stadium with natural grass and a retractable roof. In Florida, the Tampa Bay Devil Rays lost 11−6 to the Detroit Tigers in their first AL game on the same day.

MOST CLUB WINS IN A REGULAR SEASON*

Wins	Team	League	Year
116	Chicago Cubs	NL	1906
114	New York Yankees	AL	1998
111	Cleveland Indians	AL	1954
110	Pittsburgh Pirates	NL	1909
	New York Yankees	AL	1927
109	New York Yankees	AL	1961
	Baltimore Orioles	AL	1969
108	Baltimore Orioles	AL	1970
	Cincinnati Reds	NL	1975
	New York Mets	NL	1986
107	Chicago Cubs	NL	1907
	Philadelphia Athletics	AL	1931
	New York Yankees	AL	1932
106	New York Giants	NL	1904
	New York Yankees	AL	1939
	St. Louis Cardinals	NL	1942
	Atlanta Braves	NL	1998
105	New York Giants	NL	1905
	Boston Red Sox	AL	1912
	St. Louis Cardinals	NL	1943
	St. Louis Cardinals	NL	1944
	Brooklyn Dodgers	NL	1953

* National League teams played 154 games until the schedule was increased to 162 in 1962. American League teams played 154 games each season through 1960. In 1961, the schedule increased to 162 games.

3.9   **B. New York Yankees**

Graeme Lloyd pitched the New York Yankees to an 11–6 victory over the Chicago White Sox on September 4, 1998, to claim the Yankees' 100th win of the season – the earliest date any Major League team has hit the century mark. It was five days shy of the 92nd anniversary of the Chicago Cubs' 100th win of 1906 and the 44th anniversary of the Cleveland Indians' 100th win of 1954. The Yankees' win came in game 138. The Cubs' 100th victory came in their 132nd game. The Yankees finished the regular season on September 27 with an 8–3 win over the Tampa Bay Devil Rays for a 114–48 record, three wins better than the 1954 Indians' previous single-season best but two wins shy of the Cubs' 1906-record 116 wins. The Yankees were the American League East champions and went on to win their 24th World Series title.

3.10   **D. 33**

St. Louis Cardinals fans were used to seeing zeros on the scoreboard for their team in 1908. The Cardinals failed to score in 33 games that season, setting the Major League record. The Cardinals finished last in the National League at 49–105. At the other end of the spectrum were the 1932 New York Yankees. The

---

DID YOU KNOW?

The first World Series between National League and American League clubs in 1903 was a best-of-nine affair. The AL's best team, the 91–47 Boston Pilgrims, was challenged by the NL champion Pittsburgh Pirates (91–49) to the post-season series. The Pilgrims won five games to three. The series-clinching game was played on October 13, 1903, in Boston's Huntington Avenue Baseball Grounds, when Bill Dineen had a four-hit, 3–0 shutout. Dineen also had a 3–0 shutout in game two for the future Red Sox, when he limited Pittsburgh to three hits.

Yankees, who swept the Chicago Cubs in the World Series, were 107–47 in the regular season and became the first and only team to avoid a shutout in a season.

3.11   C. 26

The Brooklyn Robins and Boston Braves battled for 26 innings on May 1, 1920. The game ended in a 1–1 tie after being called because of darkness, after three hours and 50 minutes of play. The Robins threatened to end the game in the 17th inning, but failed to score with the bases loaded. Joe Oeschger of the Braves and Leon Cadore of the Robins pitched the entire game for their respective teams. The Dodgers played another 32 innings in the next two days. They lost 4–3 in 13 innings on May 2 to the Philadelphia Phillies and met the Braves again on May 3 for a 19-inning tilt that saw Boston become the 2–1 winner.

3.12   B. New York Yankees

The New York Yankees were the first to honor a player's extra-ordinary achievements by retiring his number. Lou Gehrig's number 4 was retired in 1939, the same year he was elected to the Hall of Fame. Gehrig, who appeared in 2,130 consecutive games, took himself out of the Yankees' lineup on May 2, 1939, and never played again. The Yankees saluted Gehrig on July 4 at Yankee Stadium, where Gehrig told fans in a speech that he was "the luckiest man on the face of the earth." He suffered from amyotrophic lateral sclerosis, which became known as Lou Gehrig's Disease, and died almost two years later.

3.13   B. Athletics

The Athletics began in 1901 in Philadelphia under the owner-ship and management of Connie Mack. The team was bought in 1954 by Arnold Johnson and was moved in 1955 to Kansas City, where it remained until 1967. The Athletics were then moved to their present home, Oakland, and began play there in 1968. Owner Charlie Finley had bought a majority interest in the Athletics in 1960 with plans to move the team. The Braves, meanwhile, have also called three cities home during their National League history. The team, which originated in Cincinnati, began as the Boston Red Stockings in 1876, moved to Milwaukee in 1953 and went south to Atlanta in 1966.

3.14 **C. 45**
The Major League record for most runners left on base is 45, which has been achieved twice. The Kansas City Royals and Texas Rangers combined to leave 45 runners on the bases in an 18-inning game on June 6, 1991. The Royals stranded 25, while the Rangers left 20 in the game, which lasted six hours and 20 minutes. The Royals were tired 4–3 winners. On September 11, 1974, the New York Mets left 25 and St. Louis Cardinals had 20 in a 25-inning marathon won 4–3 by the Cards.

3.15 **C. 1988**
The Chicago Cubs defeated the New York Mets 6–4 on August 9, 1988, in the first Major League night game under lights at Wrigley Field. History was delayed because the game was scheduled for the previous evening but was rained out after only three innings. The Cincinnati Reds were the first team to install permanent lighting. The switch was flipped remotely by President Franklin D. Roosevelt on May 24, 1935, before a 2–1 Reds win over the Philadelphia Phillies at Crosley Field.

3.16 **A. Colorado Rockies**
Viva béisbol! The Colorado Rockies beat the San Diego Padres 8–2 on opening day in Mexico's Estadio Monterrey, April 4, 1999. It was the first time that Major League teams opened the regular season outside the United States or Canada. It wasn't the first regular-season game in Mexico, however. On August 16, 1996, the Padres began a three-game series against the New York Mets in Monterrey but lost 15–10. The Mets rallied with seven runs in the ninth inning. The teams went south of the border to accommodate the Republican Party's national convention in San Diego.

3.17　**B. 54**

It was a scorekeeper's nightmare on September 25, 1992, when the Seattle Mariners and Texas Rangers used 54 players. The visiting Mariners, managed by Bill Plummer, were 4–3 winners of the 16-inning game and used 29 players – including 11 pitchers. Rangers manager Bobby Valentine enlisted 25 players. The teams broke a record set in 1986, when the Chicago Cubs and Houston Astros used 53 men in an 18-inning game that started September 2 and finished September 3.

3.18　**D. Chicago Cubs**

Chicago Cubs fans went to see their team play at Wrigley Field on August 25, 1922, but they left after witnessing football-style numbers on the scoreboard. The Cubs defeated the Philadelphia Phillies 26–23 in a game that ended only three hours and one minute after the opening pitch. The Cubs bounded to an early 25–6 lead after scoring ten runs in the second inning and 14 in the fourth. In that inning, Cubs outfielder Marty Callaghan came to the plate three times. He hit twice and struck out once. Philadelphia eroded the Cubs' lead and loaded the bases in the ninth inning, but it failed to tie the game.

3.19　**D. 131**

The Seattle Mariners hit 131 of their record 264 home runs in 1997 at the Kingdome in Seattle. The balance of 133 home runs was collected on the road. Ken Griffey Jr. led the team with 56 home runs. The Mariners had seven more home runs than the 1996 Baltimore Orioles, the previous record holder. The Mariners played at the Kingdome, a concrete domed stadium, for 22 years. They moved to Safeco Field, the Major Leagues' second retractable-roof stadium with a natural-grass field, on July 15, 1999.

Game Three

ESTEEMED YANKEES NAME SCRAMBLE

The New York Yankees are the all-time World Series champions, having won the fall classic an amazing 25 times in the 1900s. Unscramble the names of the following Yankee greats and arrange the letters in the correct order in the corresponding boxes. Then, use the letters in the highlighted boxes to spell a special three-word message that describes what these 11 Yankees have in common.

(*Answers are on page 120.*)

ARRBE ☐ ☐ ☐ ☐ ⬭

DORF ⬭ ☐ ☐ ☐

THUNER ☐ ☐ ☐ ☐ ⬭ ☐

HERGIG ☐ ☐ ⬭ ☐ ☐ ☐

GOMAGIDI ☐ ☐ ⬭ ⬭ ☐ ☐ ☐ ☐

NETLMA ☐ ☐ ☐ ☐ ⬭ ☐

TURH ⬭ ☐ ☐ ☐

SNOCKAJ ☐ ☐ ☐ ☐ ⬭ ☐ ☐

ZZORITU ☐ ☐ ☐ ☐ ☐ ☐ ⬭

GELNETS ☐ ☐ ☐ ☐ ☐ ☐ ⬭

FUFGRIN ☐ ☐ ⬭ ☐ ☐ ☐ ☐

4
AT THE PLATE

Baseball is unique among sports. It's not played on a rectangular surface. It's a good thing for one team if the ball goes out of play between two poles and gets lost. But it's not so good for the other team – the nine men in the field who try to control the baseball just long enough to trade places with their foes at the plate. It's the challenge of the batter (and base runner) to disrupt the dominance of the defense. Ty Cobb, the owner of baseball's best career batting average, connected with the ball and made it to first base or beyond only about 37 percent of the time. Challenge yourself to do better with this chapter's questions about baseball's hitting heroes, from the Babe to Big Mac.

(Answers are on page 41.)

4.1 What is the Major League individual record for most runs batted in during a single game?
A. Six
B. Eight
C. Ten
D. 12

4.2 Who was the first player to tie Dale Long's record for consecutive games with a home run?
A. Ken Griffey Jr.
B. Don Mattingly
C. Mark McGwire
D. Reggie Jackson

4.3 Where did Joe DiMaggio hit safely for the 56th consecutive game?

A. Yankee Stadium, New York

B. Ebbets Field, New York

C. Comiskey Park, Chicago

D. Municipal Stadium, Cleveland

4.4 What is the record for most triples in a season?

A. 26

B. 30

C. 36

D. 40

4.5 How many grand slams did Lou Gehrig hit for the career record?

A. 12

B. 23

C. 32

D. 49

4.6 What Cleveland Indians pitcher holds the Major League record for most home runs?

A. Wes Ferrell

B. Orel Hershiser

C. Bob Feller

D. Gaylord Perry

4.7 Walter James Vincent Maranville's 672 at-bats in 1922 is the record for most at-bats without a home run in a season. What was Maranville's nickname?

A. "Jimmy"

B. "Wally"

C. "Scooter"

D. "Rabbit"

4.8 Ty Cobb was the American League leader in which category a record 12 times in 13 years?
A. Batting average
B. Singles
C. Home runs
D. Strikeouts

4.9 Who broke Hank Aaron's career record for most intentional walks?
A. Cal Ripken Jr.
B. Pete Rose
C. Barry Bonds
D. George Brett

4.10 Who was the first player to win batting titles in three consecutive decades?
A. Ty Cobb
B. Ted Williams
C. Pete Rose
D. George Brett

4.11 What is the last name of the only father–son duo to hit back-to-back home runs in a Major League game?
A. Bonds
B. Ripken
C. Griffey
D. McRae

4.12 How many grand slams did Fernando Tatis have before setting a Major League record for most grand slams in one inning?
A. Zero
B. One
C. Six
D. Ten

4.13 Pete Rose recorded 14,053 at-bats in 24 years with three NL teams. For which team did he play the fewest games?
A. Cincinnati Reds
B. Philadelphia Phillies
C. New York Mets
D. Montreal Expos

4.14 Who were the Cincinnati Reds' visitors when Pete Rose made his 4,192nd base hit?
A. Philadelphia Phillies
B. San Diego Padres
C. Cleveland Indians
D. Los Angeles Dodgers

4.15 How many pinch-hits did Manny Mota have for the Major League career record?
A. 92
B. 113
C. 136
D. 150

4.16 What position was Sammy Sosa playing when Mark McGwire hit record-breaking home run number 62?
A. Right field
B. Catcher
C. Shortstop
D. Left field

4.17 How many home runs did Mark McGwire hit on the last day of the 1998 season?
A. None
B. One
C. Two
D. Three

4.18 What dubious honor does Reggie Jackson hold?
A. Most career strikeouts
B. Most ejections
C. Most times hit by a pitch
D. Most bases on balls

4.19 Jose Canseco was the first player born outside the United States to hit 400 home runs. What country is he from?
A. Cuba
B. Canada
C. Dominican Republic
D. Mexico

AT THE PLATE
Answers

4.1 **D. 12**
Jim Bottomley of the St. Louis Cardinals was the first player to record a dozen RBIs in one game. He did it on September 16, 1924, while the man whose record he broke watched from the opposing dugout. Brooklyn Robins manager Wilbert Robinson watched as Bottomley not only led the visiting Cards to a 17–3 win but also eclipsed Robinson's own single-game RBI record. As a member of the National League's Baltimore Orioles, Robinson had a record seven hits and 11 RBIs in a 25–4 win over the St. Louis Brown Stockings on June 10, 1892. Bottomley's day included a grand slam, a two-run homer, a pair of two-run singles, a one-run single and a one-run double. Almost 69 years later, another Cardinal equaled Bottomley's feat. Mark Whiten hit a grand slam, two three-run homers and a two-run shot to produce a dozen RBIs on September 7, 1993. Whiten's heroics gave his team a 15–2 victory over the Cincinnati Reds.

4.2 **B. Don Mattingly**
The Texas Rangers beat the New York Yankees 7–2 on July 18, 1987, but Don Mattingly hit a home run for the eighth

consecutive game. He tied the Major League record set by the Pittsburgh Pirates' Dale Long. Long hit eight home runs in eight games played between May 19 and 28, 1956. Mattingly, however, squeezed ten home runs into an eight-game span from July 8 to 18, 1987. Ken Griffey Jr., who made his minor-league debut a month before Mattingly's record, was the second to tie the record. On July 28, 1993, Griffey had a home run against the Minnesota Twins. He came close to setting a new record the following day, when he doubled off the center-field wall in Seattle's Kingdome.

DID YOU KNOW?

Rogers Hornsby of the St. Louis Cardinals was the first to win the triple crown more than once (1922 and 1925). The only other two-timer was Boston Red Sox star Ted Williams (1942 and 1947). The Sultan of Swat, Babe Ruth, never won a triple crown. Ruth retired in 1935 with the Boston Braves after 22 seasons with a then-record 714 career home runs, 2,213 RBIs and a .342 batting average.

4.3   D. Municipal Stadium, Cleveland

Joe DiMaggio was three-for-four with a double and two singles on July 16, 1941, to lead the New York Yankees to a 10–3 win over the Cleveland Indians at Municipal Stadium. It was the 56th consecutive game in which DiMaggio hit safely. The record is among the greatest achievements in sports. But all good things must end – which is what happened July 17. Indians pitchers Al Smith and Jim Bagby Jr. combined to retire the Yankee center fielder three times.

4.4   C. 36

John Owen "Chief" Wilson tripled 36 times in 1912 for the Pittsburgh Pirates. During the same season, "Shoeless" Joe Jackson of the Cleveland Naps set the American League record with 26.

LONGEST HITTING STREAKS

Player	Team	Games	Season
Joe DiMaggio	New York Yankees	56	1941
Willie Keeler	Baltimore Orioles	44	1897
Pete Rose	Cincinnati Reds	44	1978
Bill Dahlen	Chicago Colts	42	1894
George Sisler	St. Louis Browns	41	1922
Ty Cobb	Detroit Tigers	40	1911

4.5   B.   23

New York Yankees first baseman Lou Gehrig hit 23 grand slams during his 17-year career. His last came on August 28, 1938, on a pitch by the Philadelphia Athletics' Lee Ross.

4.6   A.   Wes Ferrell

Wes Ferrell was a threat on the mound and at the plate. He was 22–12 in 40 games pitched during 1931 for the Cleveland Indians. In the same year he hit nine home runs, the most four-baggers by a pitcher in a single season. He had a record 38 home runs during his 15-year career; 37 were made while he was listed in the batting order as a pitcher, and one was made as a pinch-hitter. Though he was a long way from Hank Aaron's 755, Ferrell did hit ten more than his brother. Hall of Fame catcher Rick Ferrell was three years older and played 18 seasons, but he managed only 28 home runs. The Ferrells were teammates on the Boston Red Sox and Washington Senators between 1934 and 1938.

4.7   D.   "Rabbit"

Walter James Vincent "Rabbit" Maranville had no home runs in the 155 games he played during 1922, even though it was his best offensive season. He batted .295, hit 15 triples and had 198 hits for the Pittsburgh Pirates. Although Maranville was only five-foot-five tall and weighed 155 pounds, he lived up to his nickname during the 23 seasons he spent in the National League. The agile defensive dynamo registered 5,133 career putouts, also a record. Maranville died at age 62, a few weeks before his 1954 election to baseball's Hall of Fame.

4.8   A.   Batting average
Detroit Tigers center fielder Ty Cobb was the American League's batting-average champion every year between 1907 and 1919, except 1916. That year, center fielder Tris Speaker of the Cleveland Indians won the only batting title of his career. Speaker had a .386 average in 1916—15 points better than Cobb's .371. Cobb's best year was 1911, when he hit .420. He retired in 1928 with a .366 career average, also a record. Cobb and Speaker were rivals on the field and were both accused in 1926 of betting on a game between their two teams seven years earlier.

4.9   C.   Barry Bonds
On July 15, 1999, Barry Bonds of the San Francisco Giants was walked intentionally for the 294th time in his career. Major League baseball's home-run king Hank Aaron was the previous record holder, with 293. Bonds received his record number of free passes in his 14th season. The son of outfielder Bobby Bonds is more proud of being the first player to hit more than 400 home runs and steal 400 bases in a career. He reached that milestone on August 23, 1998, in a 10—5 win against Florida Marlins pitcher Kirt Ojala in Miami.

4.10   D.   George Brett
Infielder George Brett won the American League batting championship three times during his 21-year career with the Kansas City Royals. Brett led the AL for the first time in 1976, his third full season, when he batted .333. He beat teammate Hal McRae, a designated hitter, by just one point. That came as a result of Brett's inside-the-park home run on October 3, 1976. Brett led

the Royals to the 1980 World Series, where they lost in six games to the Philadelphia Phillies. His .390 regular-season average was the highest of any batter since Ted Williams's .406 in 1941. He helped win a World Series in 1985 in a seven-game battle with the St. Louis Cardinals. Brett's last time atop the AL's batting chart was in 1990, when he had a .329 performance.

MOST CAREER HITS

Player	Seasons	Hits
Pete Rose	24	4,256
Ty Cobb	24	4,189
Hank Aaron	23	3,771
Stan Musial	22	3,630
Tris Speaker	22	3,514

4.11   C. Griffey

Like father, like son. Ken Griffey Sr. and Ken Griffey Jr. became the first father-and-son combination to play on the same team and hit back-to-back home runs. "Junior" was in center field and his dad in left field for the Seattle Mariners in a historic August 31, 1990, 5–2 win over the Kansas City Royals. The elder Griffey, 40, had been released a week earlier by the Cincinnati Reds and was claimed by Seattle on waivers to join his 20-year-old son. Two weeks after their first game together, they hit back-to-back home runs in the first inning of a September 14 win over the California Angels in Anaheim. Pitcher Kirk McCaskill yielded both home runs. In 2000, the Griffeys were reunited. "Junior" was traded to the Reds to join his father, the team's bench coach.

4.12 **A. Zero**

Move over, Mark McGwire! St. Louis Cardinals teammate Fernando Tatis became the tenth batter to hit a pair of grand slams in a game, but only the first to do so in the same inning! He had never hit a Major League grand slam before the third inning of an April 23, 1999, road game against pitcher Chan Ho Park and the Los Angeles Dodgers. The bases-clearing long balls by the Dominican Republic native helped St. Louis overcome the Dodgers 12–5. Tatis also set the record for most RBIs in one inning, with eight.

4.13 **D. Montreal Expos**

Bonjour. Au revoir. Of the three teams that Pete Rose played for during his career, he spent the least time with the Montreal Expos. In 1984, he got 72 hits in 95 games for Montreal. He returned to Cincinnati to become the Reds' player/manager late in the season. Rose retired from playing in 1986 but continued to manage the Reds until he was banned from baseball on August 24, 1989, by commissioner A. Bartlett Giamatti for gambling on baseball games. Rose's first tour of duty with the Reds lasted from 1963 to 1978, and he played five years for the Philadelphia Phillies.

4.14 **B. San Diego Padres**

Pete Rose's 4,192nd career hit was against the San Diego Padres, on September 11, 1985, at Cincinnati's Riverfront Stadium. It was the 57th anniversary of Ty Cobb's last game. Padres starter Eric Show surrendered the first inning single before 47,237 fans. Rose was greeted at first base by Reds coach Tommy Helms and son Pete Rose Jr., who wore a number 14 jersey like his father. The Reds' owner, Marge Schott, gave Rose a red Corvette automobile bearing the license plate PR-4192 during a special ceremony. Rose later scored both runs in the 2–0 win. The celebration to crown a new hit-king should have happened on September 8, when Rose had his 4,190th off Chicago Cubs pitcher Reggie Patterson at Wrigley Field. Cobb really retired with 4,189 hits; he was mistakenly credited with 4,191 because a score sheet from a 1910 game – in which he had a pair of hits – was counted twice. The mistake was discovered decades later, but commissioner Bowie Kuhn declined in 1981 to make the correction because so many years had passed. Rose put the matter to rest when he retired with 4,256 hits in 1986.

4.15 **D. 150**
Outfielder Manny Mota played 20 years for four teams and had 150 pinch-hits. He pinch-hit in 599 of the 1,536 games he played for the San Francisco Giants, Pittsburgh Pirates, Montreal Expos and Los Angeles Dodgers.

4.16 **A. Right field**
Sammy Sosa was playing right field for the Chicago Cubs on September 8, 1998, when Mark McGwire hit his record 62nd home run of the season – a two-out pitch in the fourth inning by Steve Trachsel – over the left field fence at St. Louis' Busch Stadium. Groundskeeper Tim Forneris retrieved the home run

MOST HOME RUNS IN A SEASON

Player	Team	Year	HR
Mark McGwire	St. Louis Cardinals	1998	70
Sammy Sosa	Chicago Cubs	1998	66
Mark McGwire	St. Louis Cardinals	1999	65
Sammy Sosa	Chicago Cubs	1999	63
Roger Maris	New York Yankees	1961	61
Babe Ruth	New York Yankees	1927	60
Babe Ruth	New York Yankees	1921	59
Jimmie Foxx	Philadelphia Athletics	1932	58
Hank Greenberg	Detroit Tigers	1938	58
Mark McGwire	Oakland/St. Louis	1997	58

ball that put McGwire ahead of late New York Yankees slugger Roger Maris, who recorded 61 homers in 1961. The ball was put on display with McGwire's jersey and bats at the Hall of Fame in Cooperstown. After crossing home plate, McGwire hugged his son Matt, a Cardinals bat boy, and climbed into the box seats near the Cardinals' dugout to greet Maris's children. McGwire was then congratulated by home run rival Sosa, who had 58 home runs. Sosa was the second to pass Maris, on September 13, with his 62nd home run against the Milwaukee Brewers at Wrigley Field. Sosa became the first player to reach 60 in two seasons with a home run on September 18, 1999, at County Stadium in Milwaukee. But McGwire overtook Sosa and ended the season with 65. His last home run was on October 3 against Trachsel and the Cubs in St. Louis.

4.17   **C. Two**
Mark McGwire had two home runs on September 27, 1998, when the Montreal Expos visited Busch Stadium. The St. Louis Cardinals' first baseman had a solo shot off Mike Thurman in the third inning for his 69th home run and a three-run blast in the seventh inning off Carl Pavano for his 70th and last of the year. Cards' fan Phil Ozersky caught the last ball, which was sold for $3.005 million at a January 1999 auction. Todd McFarlane had the winning bid for history's most expensive baseball. The Canadian comic book artist, film director and producer made it the centerpiece of his touring exhibit of baseball artifacts.

4.18   **A. Most career strikeouts**
Reggie Jackson, who hit 563 home runs during 21 years in the majors, has the most career strikeouts. He retired in 1987, with 2,597. Jackson's worst season was 1969, his second with the Athletics and the team's first in Oakland. He was fanned 171 times by opposing pitchers. That was the Major League record for most strikeouts by a left-handed batter in a season, but not the all-time one-year record. That belongs to Bobby Bonds, who had 189 in 1970, for the Giants in nearby San Francisco.

4.19 A. Cuba

Jose Canseco hit his 400th career home run for the Tampa Bay Devil Rays on April 14, 1999. Canseco was born July 2, 1964, in Cuba's capital, Havana. He became the first player born outside the United States to reach the 400 home run milestone. Coincidentally, Canseco's historic game with the Devil Rays was outside the United States at Toronto's SkyDome, against the Blue Jays – the team he played for during 1998. Canseco was the Major League home run champ in 1988 with 42, and he shared the honors with the Detroit Tigers' Cecil Fielder in 1991, when they both hit 44. Canseco and Mark McGwire were known as the "Bash Brothers" when they were teammates on the Oakland Athletics between 1986 and 1992.

DID YOU KNOW?

During Joe DiMaggio's record 56-game consecutive hitting streak in 1941, the New York Yankees star singled 56 times, had 16 doubles and four triples and hit 15 home runs between May 15 and July 16. He broke "Wee" Willie Keeler's nineteenth-century record of 44 consecutive games on July 2, with a three-run homer over the head of Boston Red Sox outfielder Ted Williams at Yankee Stadium. The bat DiMaggio used to pass Keeler was borrowed from teammate Tommy Henrich because his favorite bat was stolen from the Yankees' dugout during a rain delay on July 1.

Game Four

THE NICKNAME GAME

Baseball is an extraordinary game with some extraordinary nicknames. Match the first and last names of the record-breaking player or manager listed in the first column with the correct nickname in the second column.

(Answers are on page 120.)

1. _____ George Anderson   A. "Hack"

2. _____ Lawrence Berra   B. "Big Mac"

3. _____ Edward Ford   C. "Hoot"

4. _____ Bob Gibson   D. "Whitey"

5. _____ Mark McGwire   E. "Yogi"

6. _____ George Kelly   F. "Honus"

7. _____ Leroy Paige   G. "Casey"

8. _____ Pete Rose   H. "Highpockets"

9. _____ Edwin Snider   I. "Cy"

10. _____ Charles Stengel   J. "Satchel"

11. _____ John Wagner   K. "Charlie Hustle"

12. _____ Lloyd Waner   L. "Sparky"

13. _____ Paul Waner   M. "Duke"

14. _____ Lewis Wilson   N. "Little Poison"

15. _____ Denton Young   O. "Big Poison"

5

ON THE MOUND

The pitching mound is an 18-foot circle, one foot high at its peak and 60 ½ feet from home plate. It's an office with no walls, where the pitcher must keep total concentration despite the never-ending noise from the crowd and the occasional taunt from an opposing player. It's the focal point of the diamond, where the ball is put in play each time it leaves the hurler's hand. Unlike the case for batters, a one-third success rate just doesn't do the job for pitchers. Three batters up and three batters out are what a pitcher strives for in every inning he works. Holding the opposition batters hitless or, better yet, keeping them from advancing beyond home plate for an entire game is the ultimate goal. But a perfect game is a rare and special treat. It's your turn to aim for a perfect chapter by correctly answering the questions about baseball's greatest pitchers.

(Answers are on page 55.)

5.1 Tom Gordon's consecutive save record began and ended against which American League team?
   A. Cleveland Indians
   B. Kansas City Royals
   C. Atlanta Braves
   D. Toronto Blue Jays

5.2 Who did Jesse Orosco surpass to set a record for career pitching appearances?
   A. Cy Young
   B. Dennis Eckersley
   C. Roger Clemens
   D. Hoyt Wilhelm

5.3   What is the record for most consecutive Cy Young Awards?
A.   Three
B.   Four
C.   Five
D.   Six

5.4   For how many years did Nolan Ryan pitch to become the longest-serving Major Leaguer?
A.   15
B.   18
C.   26
D.   27

5.5   How did Anthony Young lose his record 27th consecutive game?
A.   Home run
B.   Player steals home
C.   Grand slam
D.   Winning run walked home

5.6   How many innings were there in the longest scoreless American League game?
A.   Ten
B.   12
C.   17
D.   18

5.7   Whose save record did Bobby Thigpen break on September 3, 1990?
A.   Dave Righetti
B.   Dennis Eckersley
C.   Rollie Fingers
D.   Dan Quisenberry

5.8 Against what team with a bird name did Nolan Ryan throw his record seventh no-hitter?
A. Toronto Blue Jays
B. St. Louis Cardinals
C. Baltimore Orioles
D. California Angels

5.9 Who was the first pitcher to strike out 20 batters in nine innings and set the Major League single-game record?
A. Nolan Ryan
B. Kerry Wood
C. Roger Clemens
D. Tom Seaver

5.10 How many strikeouts did Nolan Ryan pitch in the final regular season game of 1973 to set a single-season record?
A. Six
B. Ten
C. 16
D. 19

5.11 How many of Carl Hubbell's record 24 consecutive wins occurred in 1936?
A. 12
B. 16
C. 18
D. 24

5.12 What was the name of Cleveland's National League team when Cy Young made his debut there in 1890?
A. Indians
B. Spiders
C. Infants
D. Blues

5.13 Who was the first relief pitcher inducted into the Hall of Fame?
A. Hoyt Wilhelm
B. Dennis Eckersley
C. Warren Spahn
D. Rick Sutcliffe

5.14 In what year did Los Angeles Dodgers ace Orel Hershiser pitch a record 59 consecutive scoreless innings?
A. 1987
B. 1988
C. 1989
D. 1990

5.15 The Chicago Cubs' Ed Reulbach is the only pitcher in Major League history to pitch which of the following?
A. Two perfect games in a week
B. Two shutouts in one day
C. Three wins in two days
D. Four no-hitters in a season

5.16 Who is the only pitcher to throw consecutive no-hitters in Major League history?
A. Nolan Ryan
B. Johnny Vander Meer
C. Ken Forsch
D. Tom Seaver

5.17 Who are the only siblings to pitch no-hitters?
A. Ken Forsch and Bob Forsch
B. Wes Ferrell and Rick Ferrell
C. Phil Niekro and Joe Niekro
D. Greg Maddux and Mike Maddux

5.18 What Brooklyn Dodgers batter was the 27th and final out in Don Larsen's famous World Series perfect game?
A. Dale Mitchell
B. Jackie Robinson
C. Duke Snider
D. Pee Wee Reese

ON THE MOUND
Answers

5.1 **A. Cleveland Indians**
Boston Red Sox pitcher Tom Gordon's record consecutive-save streak started and ended against the Cleveland Indians. The first of 43 consecutive saves occurred on April 19, 1998, when Gordon preserved a 2–0 win at Fenway Park for Bret Saberhagen over the Indians. Gordon went the rest of the regular season without blowing a save and even made 28 appearances without allowing a batter to reach first base. But all good things must end. In Gordon's case, it happened at the worst possible time. On October 3, in game four of an American League Division Series, Gordon was called to action to protect Boston's 1–0 lead in the eighth inning. The Indians came back to win the game 2–1, thanks to David Justice's two-run double. Before the 1998 season, Gordon had only 14 saves in his ten-year career.

5.2 **B. Dennis Eckersley**
Jesse Orosco of the Baltimore Orioles made his record 1,072nd career appearance on August 17, 1999, breaking a record set by reliever Dennis Eckersley on September 26, 1998. Eckersley's mark was made the day before closing day, in a 5–2 loss to the Orioles charged to Boston Red Sox teammate Bret Saberhagen. Orosco debuted in 1979 with the New York Mets and was on the mound October 27, 1986, when the Mets beat Boston in the seventh and deciding game of the World Series.

5.3 **C. Five**

Roger Clemens won a record fifth Cy Young Award in 1998 as a member of the Toronto Blue Jays. It was the second time he won it in consecutive years. Clemens received the American League version of the most valuable pitcher award in 1986, when he registered a 24–4 record for the Boston Red Sox. He won it again in 1987 and 1991. After joining the Blue Jays in 1997, Clemens – surprise! – won the award that year. The award was established in 1956 in honor of Cy Young, baseball's winningest pitcher, who died on November 4, 1955. Brooklyn Dodger Don Newcombe was the first winner. Not until 1967, however, was the award given to pitchers in both leagues.

5.4 **D. 27**

The Major League career of Nolan Ryan began on September 11, 1966, with the New York Mets and continued with the California Angels, Houston Astros and Texas Rangers for 27 years, until September 22, 1993. The right-handed Refugio, Texas, native was 324–292 and an eight-time All-Star, but he never won a Cy Young Award. Ryan's only appearance in a World Series came in game three of the Mets' 1969 contest with the Baltimore Orioles. He went 2 ⅓ innings and registered a save for the Mets, who went on to beat the Orioles in five games. In his last appearance, the 46-year-old Ryan left the mound in Seattle's Kingdome with injured elbow ligaments after he surrendered five first-inning runs to the host Mariners. For just the third time in his career, he left a game without a strikeout. But the all-time king of the category already had 5,714.

5.5 **D. Winning run walked home**

New York Mets pitcher Anthony Young was in a bad slump in 1993. He lost his record 27th game in a row by walking home the winning Los Angeles Dodgers run on July 24, 1993. The Mets lost 5–4 in ten innings. Young's futility streak, the longest for a pitcher in Major League history, finally ended on July 28, 1993, when the Mets had a 5–4 comeback win over the expansion

COMPLETE PERFECT GAMES IN
MAJOR LEAGUE HISTORY

Date	Pitcher	Score
May 5, 1904	Cy Young	Boston Pilgrims 3 Philadelphia Athletics 0
October 2, 1908	Addie Joss	Cleveland Naps 1 Chicago White Sox 0
April 30, 1922	Charles Robertson	Chicago White Sox 2 Detroit Tigers 0
October 8, 1956	Don Larsen	New York Yankees 2 Brooklyn Dodgers 0*
June 21, 1964	Jim Bunning	Philadelphia Phillies 6 New York Mets 0
September 9, 1965	Sandy Koufax	Los Angeles Dodgers 1 Chicago Cubs 0
May 8, 1968	Jim "Catfish" Hunter	Oakland Athletics 4 Minnesota Twins 0
May 15, 1981	Len Barker	Cleveland Indians 3 Toronto Blue Jays 0
September 30, 1984	Mike Witt	California Angels 1 Texas Rangers 0
September 16, 1988	Tom Browning	Cincinnati Reds 1 Los Angeles Dodgers 0
July 28, 1991	Dennis Martinez	Montreal Expos 2 Los Angeles Dodgers 0
July 28, 1994	Kenny Rogers	Texas Rangers 4 California Angels 0
May 17, 1998	David Wells	New York Yankees 4 Minnesota Twins 0
July 18, 1999	David Cone	New York Yankees 6 Montreal Expos 0

* World Series

Florida Marlins. The Mets trailed by a run entering the ninth inning, and Young actually committed an error that allowed the Marlins to take a brief lead. The long-awaited win was Young's first since April 19, 1992.

5.6 D. 18

Detroit Tigers pitcher Ed Summers's complete-game, seven-hit performance wasn't enough to get a win on July 16, 1909, over the Washington Senators. Luckily for Summers, he didn't lose, either. Darkness forced the 18-inning game's end with the score tied 0–0 – the longest scoreless game in American League history. Summers didn't get much offensive support: Ty Cobb was hitless in seven at-bats. It was the most significant of Summers's nine shutouts over his five-year career, which included four World Series losses in 1908 and 1909. Washington's 30-year-old pitching rookie, Bill "Dolly" Gray, yielded one hit but was injured in the ninth inning.

5.7 A. Dave Righetti

When relief pitcher Bobby Thigpen emerged from the bullpen in Comiskey Park on September 3, 1990, he pitched his record 47th save of the season for the Chicago White Sox in a 4–2 win over the Kansas City Royals. The save put him ahead of New York Yankees reliever Dave Righetti on the all-time single-season list. Thigpen pitched another ten saves to end the season at 57.

5.8 A. Toronto Blue Jays

Nolan Ryan "no-hit" the Toronto Blue Jays when he pitched his Texas Rangers to a 3–0 win at Arlington, Texas, on May 1, 1991. It was the record seventh – and last – time in his career that he prevented opposing batters from hitting safely in a game. Ryan's first no-hitter came in 1973, when he pitched the California Angels to a 3–0 May 15 win over the Kansas City Royals. Exactly two months later, on July 15, 1973, he did it again in a 6–0 win over the Detroit Tigers. His other four career no-hitters came against the Minnesota Twins (1974), Baltimore Orioles (1975),

MOST CAREER PITCHING WINS

Pitcher	Seasons	Wins
Cy Young	22	511
Walter Johnson	21	417
Christy Mathewson	17	373
Grover Cleveland Alexander	20	373
Warren Spahn	21	363

MOST CAREER PITCHING LOSSES

Pitcher	Seasons	Losses
Cy Young	22	316
Jim Galvin	14	308
Nolan Ryan	27	292
Walter Johnson	21	279
Phil Niekro	24	274

Los Angeles Dodgers (1981) and Oakland Athletics (1990). Ryan also pitched a career-record 12 one-hitters, but he never achieved a perfect game.

5.9   C. Roger Clemens

At age 23 and a year after shoulder surgery, Boston Red Sox ace Roger Clemens struck out 20 Seattle Mariners on April 29, 1986, in a 3–1 win at Fenway Park. He broke the record of 19 that was held jointly by pitching greats Nolan Ryan, Tom Seaver and Steve Carlton. Clemens walked no batters and surrendered just three hits. Every Mariner who came to bat was struck out at least once; Phil Bradley was the 20th strikeout and a four-time victim. Clemens repeated the feat a decade later, when he struck out 20 Detroit Tigers on September 18, 1996. Detroit's Travis Fryman was fanned four times. Chicago Cubs rookie Kerry Wood pitched baseball's third 20-strikeout performance just two years later, on May 6, 1998, against the Houston Astros. Tom Cheney of the Washington Senators fanned 21 Baltimore Orioles in a September 12, 1962, game, but that went 16 innings. He had just 12 strikeouts after nine innings.

5.10 C. 16
Nolan Ryan struck out 16 Minnesota Twins in 11 innings on September 27, 1973, to power the California Angels to a 5–4 win at Anaheim. Rich Reese was Ryan's 383rd and final strikeout of the season. Ryan eclipsed Sandy Koufax's 1965 Major League record by one K.

5.11 B. 16
The wins kept coming for dependable New York Giants pitcher Carl Hubbell in 1936 and 1937. They didn't call him "Meal Ticket" for nothing. He pitched 24 wins in a row, starting on July 17, 1936, and continuing to May 27, 1937; 16 wins came in 1936, and the remaining eight in 1937. The two seasons were the best of Hubbell's 16-year career because he was the Major League win-leader, with 26 and 22, respectively. The left-hander finally lost 10–3 on May 31, 1937, at the Polo Grounds to the visiting Brooklyn Dodgers. Another Giants pitcher, Rube Marquard, pitched 19 consecutive wins in 1912, the most from the start of a season.

5.12 B. Spiders
Cy Young, baseball's greatest pitcher, appeared in a Major League game for the first time on August 6, 1890, playing for the Cleveland Spiders. The team defeated the Chicago White Stockings 8–1 as Young pitched a three-hitter. The Gilmore, Ohio native spent nine seasons with the Spiders, before owners Frank and Stanley Robison moved the team's best players to their National League franchise in St. Louis. The Spiders, the 1895

Temple Cup champions, were a victim of the National League's 1900 downsizing, when membership was pared from 12 teams to eight. Young also played for the Cleveland Indians and Boston's American League and National League entries. By the time he retired in 1911, he claimed many of Major League baseball's pitching records: he started 815 games and completed 749 of them. He also pitched 7,356 innings – 7,034 ⅔ as a starter – while his 511 victories and 316 losses are both records.

5.13   A.   Hoyt Wilhelm

Hoyt Wilhelm was the first reliever inducted into the Hall of Fame in 1985. A major reason for being so honored was his record of innings pitched by a reliever during a 21-year career with nine teams. He was a "fireman" for 1,871 innings and amassed 227 saves. He also racked up a record 124 relief victories. When he broke-in with the New York Giants on April 19, 1952, Wilhelm homered and tripled in his first at-bats. Wilhelm retired in 1972 at age 48, after pitching in 1,070 games, a record that stood until 1998, when Dennis Eckersley pitched in his 1,071st.

5.14   B.   1988

Orel Hershiser's dream season was 1988, when he pitched a record 59 scoreless innings in the regular season, edging former Dodger Don Drysdale's record of 58 ⅔. Hershiser broke the

RECORD CONSECUTIVE SCORELESS INNINGS

Pitcher	Team	Year	Innings
Orel Hershiser	Los Angeles Dodgers	1988	59
Don Drysdale	Los Angeles Dodgers	1968	58 ⅔
Walter Johnson	Washington Senators	1913	56
Jack Coombs	Philadelphia Athletics	1910	53
Ed Reulbach	Chicago Cubs	1908–09	50

record when he had ten shutout innings on September 28 in a 2–1 Los Angeles Dodgers loss to the San Diego Padres. The streak began on August 30, with a four-inning shutout stint in Montreal against the Expos. It continued another eight innings in post-season play. Hershiser, 23–8, led Los Angeles to the World Series and was the winning pitcher in game five, when his team clinched the championship in a 5–2 win over the Oakland Athletics on October 20. The dream only got better as Hershiser was named most valuable player of the World Series and winner of the National League's Cy Young Award.

5.15   B.   Two shutouts in one day
Ed Reulbach of the Chicago Cubs became the first pitcher in Major League history to record two shutouts on the same day. He dealt the Brooklyn Superbas 5–0 and 3–0 losses in a doubleheader on September 26, 1908. Reulbach had 40 shutouts in a 13-year career.

5.16   B.   Johnny Vander Meer
Johnny Vander Meer, the Cincinnati Reds' "Dutch Master," had two no-hitters in a row in 1938 – a feat not repeated since in the Major Leagues. It was also the first time that one pitcher threw two no-hitters in the same year. On June 11, 1938, Vander Meer shut out the Boston Bees 3–0 in Cincinnati's Crosley Field. Four days later, at Ebbets Field in Brooklyn, Vander Meer surprised the host Dodgers when he led the Reds to a 6–0 no-hit win. He surprised himself by surviving a one-out, bases loaded scenario in the ninth inning. Vander Meer was rewarded with the starting assignment in the July 6, 1938, All-Star Game in Cincinnati. The no-hitters were the crowning achievement of his career. He had an unremarkable 119–121 record during 13 years in the majors and saw only three innings of action during the Reds' 1940 World Series championship win over the Detroit Tigers.

5.17 **A. Ken Forsch and Bob Forsch**
Sacramento, California—born brothers Ken Forsch and Bob Forsch both had 16-year Major League careers and were the first brothers to pitch no-hitters. Younger brother Bob Forsch was the first. The 28-year-old "no-hit" the Philadelphia Phillies in a 5–0 win for the St. Louis Cardinals on April 16, 1978. Ken Forsch of the Houston Astros followed almost 51 weeks later, when the 32-year-old pitched a 6–0 win over the Atlanta Braves on April 7, 1979. Bob Forsch won the sibling rivalry when he had his second career no-hitter on September 26, 1983, in a 3–0 Cardinals win over the Montreal Expos in St. Louis.

5.18 **A. Dale Mitchell**
On October 8, 1956, Don Larsen of the New York Yankees pitched the only perfect game in post-season history. He shut out the Brooklyn Dodgers 2–0 in the fifth game of what would be the last crosstown World Series between teams from the Bronx and Brooklyn. Larsen's heroics put the Yankees one win away from the championship, after the team had started the series with a pair of losses. The tension mounted at Yankee Stadium in the top of the ninth inning as Dale Mitchell, pinch-hitting for Dodgers starting pitcher Sal Maglie, came to the plate with two out. Mitchell, a two-time All-Star with the Cleveland Indians, was called out on strikes by home plate umpire Babe Pinelli to end the game. It was the seventh strikeout for Larsen and last Major League at-bat of Mitchell's 11-year career. Larsen's eight-team, 14-year career ended in 1967 with an unspectacular 81–91 record.

Game Five

THEY SAID IT

Throughout history, record-breaking baseball personalities have rarely been at a loss for words. Some are downright philosophical about their sport. Match the pearls of wisdom with the players who uttered them.

(*Answers are on page 120.*)

A. Ernie Banks   I. Yogi Berra
B. Pete Rose   J. Reggie Jackson
C. Babe Ruth   K. Ty Cobb
D. Lou Gehrig   L. "Wee" Willie Keeler
E. Joe DiMaggio   M. Cal Ripken Jr.
F. Hank Aaron   N. Roger Maris
G. Sammy Sosa   O. Casey Stengel
H. Tommy Lasorda

1. _____ "I have only one superstition. I make sure to touch all the bases when I hit a home run."

2. _____ "Guessing what the pitcher is going to throw is 80 percent of being a successful hitter. The other 20 percent is just execution."

3. _____ "It ain't over 'til it's over."

4. _____ "Now they talk on the radio about the records set by Ruth and DiMaggio and Henry Aaron. But they rarely mention mine. Do you know what I have to show for the 61 home runs? Nothing, exactly nothing."

5. _____ "I'm the straw that stirs the drink."

6. _____ "Cut me and I'll bleed Dodger blue."

7. _____ "The great trouble with baseball today is that most of the players are in the game for the money and that's it – not for the love of it, the excitement of it, the thrill of it."

8. _____ "Baseball has been very good to me."

9. _____ "I'd walk through hell in a gasoline suit to keep playing baseball."

10. _____ "Whether your name is Gehrig, or Ripken, DiMaggio or Robinson, or that of some youngster who picks up his bat or puts on his glove, you are challenged by the game of baseball to do your very best, day in and day out, and that's all I've ever tried to do."

11. _____ "Good pitching will always stop good hitting and vice versa."

12. _____ "It's a great day for a ball game. Let's play two."

13. _____ "You always get a special kick on opening day, no matter how many you go through. You look forward to it like a birthday party when you're a kid. You think something wonderful is going to happen."

14. _____ "Hit 'em where they ain't."

15. _____ "I consider myself the luckiest man on the face of the earth."

6

ON THE BASES, IN THE FIELD

A trip around the bases is 360 feet, a distance the batter wants to travel each time he steps to the plate (unless his manager offers different instructions). Between the foul lines, there's 90,000 square feet of real estate where the defense tries to prevent the ball from trespassing. Home-run hitters and strikeout pitchers get all the glory, but the real hard work is done on the bases and in the field. A lot goes on between the lines and the bags. Test your knowledge of the infielders, outfielders and baserunners who add extra excitement to baseball.

(*Answers are on page 70.*)

6.1 **What position did Cal Ripken Jr. play on September 6, 1995, in his record-breaking 2,131st consecutive game?**
A. Second base
B. Third base
C. Shortstop
D. Designated hitter

6.2 **Who stole the most bases in a season?**
A. Lou Brock
B. Rickey Henderson
C. Tim Raines
D. Vince Coleman

6.3 **How many consecutive bases did Vince Coleman steal without being caught?**
A. 25
B. 40
C. 50
D. 75

6.4 Which California team did Steve Garvey play with when he set records for most consecutive games without an error?
A. Los Angeles Dodgers
B. San Diego Padres
C. Oakland Athletics
D. San Francisco Giants

6.5 Darren Lewis played his first Major League game in 1990. In what year did he commit his first error?
A. 1990
B. 1992
C. 1994
D. 1995

6.6 What position did Major League double-play king Mickey Vernon play?
A. Catcher
B. First baseman
C. Shortstop
D. Center field

6.7 Players from teams in which city share the record for most unassisted double plays in a season?
A. New York
B. Chicago
C. Los Angeles
D. St. Louis

6.8 Who set the record for the least errors by a shortstop in a season?
A. Cal Ripken Jr.
B. Joe Tinker
C. Eddie Brinkman
D. Ernie Banks

6.9 Which Chicago White Sox catcher caught the most no-hitters in history?
A. Carlton Fisk
B. Ray Schalk
C. Billy Sullivan Sr.
D. Gabby Hartnett

6.10 Which National League team did Ron LeFlore play with in 1980, when he led the league in stolen bases?
A. New York Mets
B. Chicago Cubs
C. San Francisco Giants
D. Montreal Expos

6.11 Who holds career and single-season records for stealing home?
A. Lou Brock
B. Ty Cobb
C. Vince Coleman
D. Pete Rose

6.12 In what stadium did the most famous catch of Willie Mays's career happen?
A. Polo Grounds
B. Municipal Stadium
C. Shea Stadium
D. Candlestick Park

6.13 Jake Beckley spent one season in which league?
A. Players League
B. American League
C. National Football League
D. National League

6.14 Ivan Rodriguez stole 35 bases in his ninth season with the Texas Rangers. How many bases did he steal during his first eight seasons?
A. 35
B. 52
C. 76
D. 89

6.15 Who was the first baseman in the Chicago Cubs' legendary double-play combination who also managed the team to a record 116 regular season wins in 1906?
A. Frank Chance
B. Joe Tinker
C. Jiggs Donahue
D. Fred Merkle

6.16 Which brothers were two of the three outs in Jimmy Cooney's unassisted triple play on May 30, 1927?
A. Joe and Tommie Sewell
B. Paul and Lloyd Waner
C. Vince and Joe DiMaggio
D. Rick and Wes Ferrell

6.17 The Minnesota Twins turned two triple plays in one game against the Boston Red Sox. Which Twins third baseman started both plays on groundouts?
A. Harmon Killebrew
B. Steve Braun
C. Gary Gaetti
D. Ron Coomer

6.18 Which Hall of Fame outfielder involved in a record two triple-steals in one game was born Aloys Szymanski?
A. Milo Allison
B. Mel Simons
C. Mickey Cochrane
D. Al Simmons

ON THE BASES, IN THE FIELD
Answers

6.1 **C. Shortstop**

Cal Ripken Jr. made his record-breaking 2,131st consecutive game a memorable one. On September 6, 1995, the Baltimore Orioles' shortstop surpassed the New York Yankees' iron-man Lou Gehrig for the Major League record of most consecutive games played. He was saluted in a 22-minute ceremony in the middle of the fifth inning, when the game became official. Ripken had two hits, including a fourth-inning home run, and a double play in the 4–2 win over the California Angels at Camden Yards. Ripken debuted with the Orioles on August 10, 1981, played alongside brother Billy for 659 games and was managed for 169 games by father Cal Ripken Sr. The 1982 rookie of the year was also most valuable player of the 1983 World Series. The iron-man's streak finally ended at 2,632, when the Orioles hosted the New York Yankees in their last home game of the 1998 season. The September 20 game was the first one Ripken missed since May 29, 1982.

6.2 **B. Rickey Henderson**

Rickey Henderson is Major League baseball's greatest single-season base thief. As a member of the Oakland Athletics, he stole four bases – including his record-setting 119th of the season – on August 27, 1982. The historic stolen base was his first of the game and happened on a pitchout by Milwaukee Brewers hurler George "Doc" Medich in the third inning of the A's 5–4 loss. Medich walked Henderson with two out on four straight pitches and threw to first baseman Cecil Cooper four times to keep Henderson on first. Henderson was called safe at second when umpire Mike Reilly said he beat a throw from catcher Ted Simmons to shortstop Robin Yount. Henderson pulled out the base and walked to home plate for a ceremony to commemorate his achievement. Henderson stole second in the sixth and both second and third in the eighth. He surpassed St. Louis Cardinals stolen-base specialist Lou Brock, who had 118 in 1974. Henderson finished the year with 130. However, he was caught stealing a record 42 times.

MOST STOLEN BASES IN A SEASON			
Player	**Team**	**Year**	**Total**
Rickey Henderson	Oakland Athletics	1982	130
Lou Brock	St. Louis Cardinals	1974	118
Vince Coleman	St. Louis Cardinals	1985	110
Vince Coleman	St. Louis Cardinals	1987	109
Rickey Henderson	Oakland Athletics	1983	108

6.3 C. 50

Vince Coleman was seemingly invincible from the late stages of the 1988 season to mid-1989. He stole a record 50 consecutive bases for the St. Louis Cardinals without being caught from September 18, 1988, to July 26, 1989. Four years earlier, in 1985, Coleman led the Major Leagues when he stole a rookie-record 110 bases in 151 games. He had only one in the National League Championship Series against the Los Angeles Dodgers and was unable to play in the World Series against the rival Kansas City Royals. He was injured before game four of the NLCS in a freak accident, when his left leg was run over by the automatic tarp at St. Louis' Busch Stadium.

6.4   **B.   San Diego Padres**

San Diego Padres first baseman Steve Garvey went 193 consecutive games without an error – a record for an infielder – from the second game of a June 26, 1983, doubleheader to April 14, 1985. During the streak, he successfully accepted 1,623 consecutive chances. The feat encompassed the entire 1984 season, when Garvey went 159 games without an error (also a record). The streak ended on April 15, 1985, when he dropped a foul pop-up in the ninth inning of an 8–3 loss to the San Francisco Giants in San Diego. Garvey began his career with the Los Angeles Dodgers in 1969.

6.5   **C.   1994**

Darren Lewis wasn't a grizzled vet, but he wasn't a rookie either, when he committed his first error. It took until 1994 for the Berkeley, California, native, who debuted on August 21, 1990, in an Oakland Athletics uniform. He joined the crosstown San Francisco Giants the next season and went errorless through June 29, 1994. Montreal Expos first baseman Cliff Floyd caused the streak to end when Lewis was charged with a fielding error in San Francisco on June 30, 1994. The errorless string lasted 392 games, a record for any player. His 938 consecutive chances accepted without an error is also a record for an outfielder.

6.6   **B.   First baseman**

Mickey Vernon is credited with the most double plays in a Major League career. The first baseman turned 2,044 in 19 years with the Washington Senators, Cleveland Indians, Boston Red Sox and Milwaukee Braves. Vernon, who debuted in 1939, missed the 1944 and 1945 seasons while serving in the U.S. military in World War II. He retired in 1960 with the Pittsburgh Pirates after seeing action in nine games as a pinch-hitter.

6.7   **D.   St. Louis**

The Major League record for most unassisted double plays in a season belongs to a St. Louis player. In fact, it's shared by two

St. Louis first basemen who played for different teams in different leagues during different decades. The St. Louis Browns' Jim Bottomley set the American League record of eight unassisted double plays in 1936. A quarter century later, in 1961, Bill White of the St. Louis Cardinals made eight.

6.8   **A. Cal Ripken Jr.**
Cal Ripken Jr. played in all 161 games in 1990 for the Baltimore Orioles and was charged with only three errors as a shortstop, breaking Eddie Brinkman's 1972 record of seven in 156 games with the Detroit Tigers. In 1990, from April 14 until the first game of a July 28 doubleheader, Ripken successfully accepted 431 chances, the most consecutive chances without an error in a single season.

6.9   **B. Ray Schalk**
Chicago White Sox catcher Ray Schalk helped four pitchers make Major League history. He caught the most no-hitters of any catcher. His proudest moment came when he caught Charles Robertson's perfect game, a 2–0 win over the Detroit Tigers on April 30, 1922. Schalk also recorded 226 double plays, the most for any catcher. That's because he didn't restrict his defensive heroics to home plate. He often dropped his mask and helped at first or third and even made the odd putout at second base.

6.10   **D. Montreal Expos**
Outfielder Ron LeFlore spent just one season in the National League, but it was worth it. During his 139 games with the Montreal Expos in 1980, he stole 97 bases to become the first player to lead both leagues in base-stealing. Two years earlier, in 1978, he stole 68 bases as a member of his hometown Detroit Tigers.

6.11   **B. Ty Cobb**
Ty Cobb did a lot of things in his career for the Detroit Tigers and was considered a hard-nosed competitor who had a penchant

for scoring the hard way. Cobb recorded the most career steals of home from first base and made the single-season record for stealing home. For that reason, pitchers were constantly looking over their shoulder at Cobb. He stole home from first base once in each of 1909 and 1911 and twice in 1912. He stole home another six times in 1912 for the single-season record of eight. He retired with 50 steals of home.

6.12   **A. Polo Grounds**

Willie Mays is the putout king of the outfield. He made 7,095 putouts in 2,843 games during his 22-year National League career with the New York Giants, San Francisco Giants and New York Mets. That figure includes his most famous play, known simply as "The Catch." It happened on September 29, 1954, in game one of the World Series between Mays's New York Giants and the Cleveland Indians at the roomy Polo Grounds in New York. Vic Wertz of the Indians clobbered a 460-foot shot to deep center field off relief pitcher Don Liddle in the top of the eighth inning. Mays got under the ball and stunned fans of both teams by recording the first out and preventing the Indians from breaking a 2–2 tie. The Giants scored three runs in the bottom of the tenth for a 5–2 win and went on to upset the Indians in four straight games for the championship.

6.13   **A. Players League**

Jake Beckley played for 20 years, which is a worthy achievement, but not unique. What set the first baseman apart was his overwhelming number of putouts (23,696). Beckley played for National League teams in Pittsburgh, New York, Cincinnati and St. Louis and in Pittsburgh's entry in the short-lived Players League, the Burghers. That was in 1890, when Beckley had 22 triples to co-lead the eight-team, renegade league in that category. Disgruntled National League and American Association players who were opposed to salary limits by team owners formed the PL, which lasted just one season.

6.14 **A. 35**

It was a very good year for Texas Rangers catcher Ivan Rodriguez in 1999. He stole as many bases in his ninth year as he had in his previous eight Major League seasons. The Puerto Rican hit 25 home runs and stole 35 bases. His totals vaulted him into the record books as the first catcher to hit 20 or more home runs and steal 20 or more bases in a season. He got the record when he stole second base in an August 14, 1999, game against the Chicago White Sox at Comiskey Park. Rodriguez' offensive and defensive performance during the season earned him the American League's most valuable player award. He was the first catcher honored since New York Yankee Thurman Munson was named MVP in 1976.

6.15 **A. Frank Chance**

First baseman Frank Chance took over at age 27 from manager Frank Selee in 1905 and continued to play in the Chicago Cubs' formidable "Tinker to Evers to Chance" infield with second baseman Johnny Evers and shortstop Joe Tinker. Selee was suffering from tuberculosis when he left the 37–28, fourth-place team. Under Chance, the team went 55–33 and finished third with a 92–61 record. But the best was yet to come. In 1906, Chance took the team Selee had assembled and set a single-season record for wins, with 116; the Cubs lost only 36 games. Chance even led the major leagues with 57 stolen bases. But it wasn't the perfect season; the Cubs lost the World Series in six games to the crosstown Chicago White Sox. Chance's Cubs won four National League pennants in five years and were World Series champions in 1907 and 1908.

6.16 **B. Paul and Lloyd Waner**

Paul Waner of the Pittsburgh Pirates hit a line drive to Chicago Cubs shortstop Jimmy Cooney on May 30, 1927, for the first out of the fourth inning – and the play. Cooney touched second base to get Waner's brother Lloyd out and then ended the inning when he tagged Clyde Barnhart, who was heading to second from first. Cooney knew what it was like to be in the Waners' shoes. As a St. Louis Cardinal, he was one of the victims in Pittsburgh shortstop Glenn Wright's unassisted triple play on May 7, 1925. The day after Cooney's triple play, Johnny Neun of the Detroit Tigers had one of his own against the Cleveland Indians. It was the first time that unassisted triple plays happened on consecutive days.

6.17 C. Gary Gaetti

Minnesota Twins third baseman Gary Gaetti started both triple plays on July 17, 1990, against the Boston Red Sox. On both occasions Gaetti tagged third base and threw to Al Newman at second base, who then sent the ball to first baseman Kent Hrbek. Boston's Tom Brunansky hit into the triple-killing in the fourth inning when the bases were loaded. In the eighth, Jody Reed was at the plate with runners on first and third. Despite the Twins' defensive record, the Red Sox were 1–0 winners. In a game between the same two teams the next day, Minnesota had six double plays and Boston four, to set a nine-inning record of ten. The Twins were one shy of tying the record of seven, set August 14, 1942, when New York Yankee short-stop Phil Rizutto and second baseman Joe Gordon made seven to help beat the Philadelphia Athletics 11–2. First baseman Curt Blefary was involved in all seven of the Houston Astros' record-tying double plays on May 4, 1969, in a 3–1 win over the visiting San Francisco Giants.

6.18 D. Al Simmons

Milwaukee native Al Simmons was born Aloys Szymanski on May 22, 1902. This son of Polish immigrants was part of two triple steals in one game. On July 25, 1930, the Philadelphia Athletics did it twice in the first and fourth innings of a 14–1 victory over the Cleveland Indians. Simmons, Bing Miller and Dib Williams were involved in the first inning burglary. Mickey Cochrane, Simmons and Jimmie Foxx did it in the fourth.

Did You Know?

Lou Gehrig started his consecutive-games streak on June 1, 1925, when he replaced first baseman Wally Pipp after pinch-hitting in the eighth inning for Paul Wanninger. The next day, Gehrig started in place of Pipp after the regular was hit on the head in batting practice. Pipp had 15 seasons in the Major Leagues and played 1,872 games. When Gehrig replaced him, he had been the Yankees' starting first baseman since 1915. He finished his career with three years as a member of the Cincinnati Reds. Gehrig was three-for-five in the Yankees 8–5 win over the Washington Senators and would play in every single game over the next 14 seasons until an April 30, 1939, game against the Senators in Washington, D.C. That was the 2,130th and last game for Gehrig, who was suffering from a disease that would kill him almost two years later and come to be known as Lou Gehrig's Disease. He pulled himself from the lineup ("for the good of the team," he said) of a May 2 game in Detroit against the Tigers. Elsworth "Babe" Dahlgren took his spot and hit a homer and a double in the 22–2 Yankees win. Dahlgren played 1,137 games over 12 years for the Yankees and seven other teams. Gehrig's seemingly invincible record was eclipsed by Cal Ripken Jr. in 1995.

Game Six

WONDER YEARS

Match the record incident with the year it happened.

(*Answers are on page 120.*)

Years

A. 1985	E. 1947	I. 1941	M. 1928
B. 1903	F. 1930	J. 1914	N. 1939
C. 1961	G. 1994	K. 1906	O. 1974
D. 1998	H. 1956	L. 1911	

Clues

1. _____ Mark McGwire hits 70 home runs.
2. _____ World Series is canceled by a players' strike.
3. _____ Pete Rose becomes career hit leader.
4. _____ Hank Aaron breaks Babe Ruth's career home run record.
5. _____ Roger Maris hits 61 home runs.
6. _____ Don Larsen has a perfect World Series game.
7. _____ The Dodgers' Jackie Robinson breaks the color barrier and is named rookie of the year.
8. _____ Joe DiMaggio hits safely in 56 consecutive games.
9. _____ Lou Gehrig retires after playing 2,130 consecutive games.
10. _____ Hack Wilson has 191 RBIs.
11. _____ Ty Cobb gets hit number 4,189.
12. _____ Babe Ruth makes his Major League debut with the Boston Red Sox.
13. _____ Cy Young ends his career with 511 wins.
14. _____ The Chicago Cubs have a record 116-win season.
15. _____ The first World Series is played between Boston and Pittsburgh.

7
SEVENTH INNING STRETCH

You've reached the seventh chapter. It's an ideal time to take a break, sing "Take Me Out to the Ball Game" and do your best to answer some offbeat true-or-false questions. Root, root, root for yourself, because there are a few change-ups and curveballs among this set of questions. Win or lose, the answers are guaranteed to fascinate.

(Answers are on page 81.)

7.1 Hank Aaron holds not only the Major League baseball record for most career home runs, but also the world professional baseball record. **True or False?**

7.2 The all-time Major League baseball attendance record was set at a 1959 exhibition game in Los Angeles. **True or False?**

7.3 A pair of inside-the-park home runs was hit on August 27, 1977, at Yankee Stadium. **True or False?**

7.4 The longest game in Major League history, by length of time (not number of innings), ended before midnight on the day it started. **True or False?**

7.5 The first Major League baseball game on radio was broadcast from Pittsburgh. **True or False?**

7.6 Joe DiMaggio hit safely in 56 consecutive Major League games for the New York Yankees. He had an even longer streak in the Pacific Coast League for his hometown San Francisco Seals. **True or False?**

7.7 The lyricist of "Take Me Out to the Ball Game" was a New York Giants player. **True or False?**

7.8 Joel Youngblood hit safely for the New York Mets and Montreal Expos on the same day. **True or False?**

7.9 In 1961, Roger Maris broke Babe Ruth's single-season home run record and had the best batting average in the majors. **True or False?**

7.10 The shortest player in Major League history was a member of the St. Louis Browns. **True or False?**

7.11 Country music's Garth Brooks and basketball's Michael Jordan played for the Chicago Cubs in the 1990s. **True or False?**

7.12 Pitchers nicknamed "Lefty" have won the triple crown four times. **True or False?**

7.13 No Major League team has won nine consecutive pennants. **True or False?**

7.14 A woman has never been drafted by a Major League baseball club. **True or False?**

7.15 Don Larsen, who pitched the only perfect game in World Series history, was part of the largest trade in Major League baseball history. **True or False?**

7.16 Major Leaguers Jackie Robinson and Frank Robinson were brothers. **True or False?**

7.17 The 1989 World Series was the first to be disrupted by an earthquake. **True or False?**

7.18 Bert Campaneris played all nine positions for the Kansas City Royals once in 1965. **True or False?**

SEVENTH INNING STRETCH
Answers

7.1 **False**

Sadaharu Oh of Tokyo's Yomiuri Giants hit 868 home runs during his career in Japan's Central League. He retired with 113 more homers than Hank Aaron, the Major League record holder with 755. Oh moved ahead of Aaron on September 3, 1977. His 756th home run was a solo shot in the third inning of an 8–1 win over the Yakult Swallows. Oh had his home runs in 9,250 at-bats – 3,114 fewer than Aaron. Every year from 1962 to 1977, except 1975, Oh led the Central League in home runs. His best year was 1964, when he hit a league-record 55. Oh led the Giants to nine consecutive Japan Series championships from 1965 to 1973. Aaron hit 44 three times (1957, 1963 and 1966) and 39 once (1967), to take the National League crown. Aaron's only World Series championship was in 1957, when the Milwaukee Braves beat the New York Yankees in seven games.

7.2 **True**

The all-time attendance record of 93,103 for a Major League baseball game happened on May 7, 1959, at Los Angeles Memorial Coliseum. The New York Yankees beat the Los Angeles Dodgers 6–2 in a charity exhibition honoring ex–Brooklyn Dodgers catcher Roy Campanella, a three-time National League most valuable player. Campanella's career ended when he was paralyzed in a car crash on January 28, 1958. The Dodgers moved from Brooklyn and played their first west coast game with the former New York Giants in San Francisco on April 15, 1958. San Francisco shut out Los Angeles 8–0 at Seals Stadium in front of 23,192 fans.

7.3   **True**

For the first time in Major League history, inside-the-park home runs were hit on consecutive pitches, at Yankee Stadium on August 27, 1977. Texas Rangers Toby Harrah and Elliott "Bump" Wills traveled around the bases without the ball leaving the park on back-to-back pitches by New York Yankees rookie Ken Clay. With one out in the seventh inning and two men on base, Harrah hit Clay's pitch to the right-field wall, forcing Lou Piniella to jump. But the ball hit Piniella's glove and bounced off the wall. Piniella fell to the ground but returned to play in time for Wills to follow with a long ball to deep center field. That blast deflected off Mickey Rivers' glove. The Rangers were 8–2 winners.

7.4   **False**

The Chicago White Sox and Milwaukee Brewers dueled 25 innings, until a Harold Baines home run ended the marathon eight-hour and six-minute game to give Chicago a 7–6 win at Comiskey Park. It began on May 8, 1984, but was suspended at 1:05 a.m. on May 9, after 17 innings, because of a curfew. The teams played another eight innings later on May 9. Tom Seaver got credit for the win. Brewers pitcher Chuck Porter was the loser. The teams were one inning away from tying the record for longest Major League game by innings. That record was set on May 1, 1920, at Braves Field in Boston. The Brooklyn Robins and Braves meeting ended in a 1–1, 26-inning tie.

7.5   **True**

KDKA in Pittsburgh was the first radio station to broadcast a Major League baseball game. The airwaves came alive on August 5, 1921, with the sounds of a Pirates game against Pennsylvania rival Philadelphia Phillies. Harold Arlin, from a field-level box seat, described the Pirates' one-hour and 57-minute 8–5 win live from Forbes Field. Another 18 years passed before baseball was televised. NBC's experimental W2XBS station carried a Cincinnati Reds–Brooklyn Dodgers doubleheader live from Ebbets Field on August 26, 1939. The teams split the twin bill as Dodgers radio broadcaster Red Barber provided play-by-play. The ratings were understandably low; there were only 400 TV sets in the Big Apple at the time.

7.6 **True**

Joe DiMaggio hit safely in 56 consecutive New York Yankees' games in 1941. This figure still stands as one of the greatest records in professional sport, but it wasn't DiMaggio's personal best. He hit safely in 61 consecutive games in 1933 with the Pacific Coast League's San Francisco Seals.

7.7 **False**

"Take Me Out to the Ball Game" was written by Jack Norworth, a veteran of the vaudeville stage in New York. The chorus of Norworth's song is traditionally played in the seventh-inning stretch. It's the most-played and most-recorded of all baseball songs and widely considered baseball's anthem. When Norworth wrote it in 1908, he had never seen a baseball game. He spotted a New York Giants subway billboard reading "Baseball Today – Polo Grounds" during a trolley ride. That prompted him to write the lyrics, which were put to music by Albert Von Tilzer.

7.8 **True**

Center fielder Joel Youngblood was a busy man on August 4, 1982. He was the first major leaguer to hit in two different cities for two different teams on the same day. He was traded from the New York Mets to the Montreal Expos. He hit a two-run single in the third inning against the Cubs' Ferguson Jenkins in what would be his final game as a Met, a 7–4 New York win. Youngblood was traded for Montreal Expos pitcher Tom Gorman and left Wrigley Field to catch a flight to Philadelphia. He joined his new team in time to debut as a right fielder and hit a single off Phillies pitcher Steve Carlton in the 5–4 Montreal loss at Veterans Stadium.

7.9 **False**

Roger Maris's 61st home run, on October 1, 1961, against the Boston Red Sox, gave the American League champion New York Yankees a 1–0 win to finish the regular season. The fourth-inning dinger off pitcher Tracy Stallard broke Babe Ruth's single-season record from 1927. Maris's .269 batting average was well below the .361 registered by the Major Leagues' batting champion, Norm Cash of the Detroit Tigers. The only season a player hit the most home runs and led in batting average was 1956. Maris's teammate Mickey Mantle had 52 home runs and a .353 average that year. Mantle also had 130 RBIs to win the AL's triple crown.

7.10 **True**

All three feet and seven inches of Eddie Gaedel came to the plate just once for the St. Louis Browns, on August 19, 1951, against the Detroit Tigers. The 26-year-old Chicago native with the tiny strike zone was walked on four pitches by Bob Cain and replaced by pinch-runner Jim Delsing in the first inning of the second half of a doubleheader. Gaedel was the shortest player in Major League history, thanks to his hiring by Browns owner Bill Veeck, who was called the "P.T. Barnum of baseball." Gaedel's appearance in the game and his unique jersey number, $\frac{1}{8}$, gave him a small niche in baseball history.

7.11 **False**

Country music superstar Garth Brooks broke records for selling millions of compact discs and concert tickets, but he wasn't so lucky on the baseball diamond. He put down his guitar and microphone and picked up a bat and glove for spring training in 1999. He had just one hit in 22 at-bats in Cactus League play for the San Diego Padres. The 37-year-old's lone single was on March 21, 1999, in an 11–8 loss to the Chicago White Sox. He returned to his music career in time for the regular season. Basketball legend Michael Jordan did marginally better when he temporarily retired from basketball to become a baseball player in 1994. He was 3-for-20 at the plate for the White Sox in spring training. Jordan was assigned to Chicago's double A affiliate in Birmingham, Alabama, and compiled a .202 batting average. The Chicago Bulls were glad when he returned to the National Basketball Association in 1995: Jordan led them to a second trio of NBA championships from 1996 to 1998.

7.12   True

Robert "Lefty" Grove and Vernon "Lefty" Gomez both led the American League in wins, strikeouts and earned run average twice. Grove won the triple crown in 1930 and 1931 for the Philadelphia Athletics. Gomez, of the New York Yankees, was the triple crown winner in 1934 and 1937. Grover Cleveland Alexander, however, is the all-time triple crown champion. He won it in the National League three times with the Philadelphia Phillies (1915, 1916 and 1917) and once with the Chicago Cubs (1920).

7.13   True

No Major League baseball team has won nine consecutive pennants. But the Homestead Grays won nine flags in a row in the Negro National League from 1937 to 1945. They won the Negro League World Series in 1943 and 1944. The team, which started in Pittsburgh and played at Forbes Field, also called Washington, D.C.'s Griffith Stadium home. Among the Grays' stars were catcher Josh Gibson and first baseman Buck Leonard, a duo that was compared to Babe Ruth and Lou Gehrig, respectively. Another prominent team in the Negro leagues was the Kansas City Monarchs, which included greats like Buck O'Neil, Satchel Paige and Jackie Robinson. Until Robinson debuted in 1947 for the Brooklyn Dodgers, African-Americans were not allowed to play Major League baseball. They had their own leagues from the 1920s to the 1950s because racist policies kept them from being full and equal members of Major League baseball and American society. Many Major League players supported segregation because they privately feared that some of the Negro leagues' top stars would take their jobs.

7.14 **False**

Karey Schueler was first woman claimed in Major League baseball's annual draft. The Chicago White Sox made Schueler their 43rd pick in the 1993 draft. Her father was White Sox general manager Ron Schueler. No woman has ever played a regular-season game in either the National or American leagues. But long before Bo Jackson and Deion Sanders made headlines as dual-sport athletes in the 1980s, Babe Didrikson Zaharias pitched one inning for the Philadelphia Athletics against the Brooklyn Dodgers in a March 20, 1934, spring training game. Zaharias, a world-class golfer, basketball player and track and field athlete, issued one walk but yielded no hits. From 1943 to 1954, women did have a league of their own, called the All-American Girls Professional Baseball League. It was the brainchild of Chicago Cubs owner Phillip Wrigley. Helen Callaghan, a Canadian who played for the Minneapolis Millerettes, Fort Wayne Daisies and Kenosha Comets, was the only player whose son had a Major League career: Casey Candaele was an outfielder with the Montreal Expos, Houston Astros and Cleveland Indians.

7.15 **True**

The largest trade in Major League baseball history happened after the 1954 season. In a two-part deal that began on November 18, the New York Yankees and Baltimore Orioles exchanged 17 identified players and one to be named later. The Yankees received pitcher Mike Blyzka, outfielder Jim Fridley, shortstop Billy Hunter, first baseman Dick Kryhoski, pitcher Don Larsen, catcher Darrell Johnson and pitcher Bob Turley. The Orioles received pitcher Harry Byrd, outfielder Ted Del Guercio, second baseman Don Leppert, pitcher Jim McDonald, outfielder Bill Miller, shortstop Willie Miranda, infielder Kal Segrist, catchers Hal Smith and Gus Triandos and outfielder Gene Woodling. Turley led the Yankees to the AL pennant in 1955, with a 17–13 record. In 1956, Larsen pitched the only perfect game in World Series history.

7.16 False

Jackie Robinson, the first black American player in Major League baseball, and Frank Robinson, MLB's first black American manager, were not related. Jackie, a native of Cairo, Georgia, broke the "color barrier" when he debuted with the Brooklyn Dodgers and went 0-for-3 on April 15, 1947. He was voted baseball's first rookie of the year. Beaumont, Texas–born Frank was the 1956 National League rookie of the year. He made his debut as a playing manager for the Cleveland Indians on April 8, 1975, at Municipal Stadium, with a first-inning home run in a 5–3 win over the New York Yankees.

7.17 True

The Oakland Athletics led 2–0 when the World Series shifted across San Francisco Bay to Candlestick Park on October 17, 1989. Before the first pitch could be thrown, an earthquake measuring 7.1 on the Richter scale rumbled through northern California. The San Francisco Giants, the Athletics and their fans were forced to evacuate the stadium. The cancellation of the series was considered while Bay Area residents tried to recover from the devastating natural disaster, which killed 67. But the series resumed ten days later, on October 27, with a 13–7 Oakland win at Candlestick. The A's completed the sweep a day later, on October 28, by winning 9–6.

7.18 True

Kansas City Athletics shortstop Bert Campaneris was moved around the field and scorecard on September 8, 1965, when he played all nine positions in a 13-inning, 5–3 loss to the California Angels. Campaneris didn't go the distance, however. His last position was catcher, but he left in the ninth inning after being injured in a home-plate collision with Ed Kirkpatrick. Campaneris had already reached his goal of becoming the first to play all nine positions in one game.

Game Seven

The Century Club Word Search

A regular season with 100 or more wins is a big achievement for a team. The Boston Beaneaters (later known as the Braves) started baseball's "century club" when they led the National League with a 102−48 won−lost record in 1892. The 1906 Chicago Cubs had an all-time best 116−36. The New York Yankees came close when they finished 114−48 in 1998, the team's record 15th season in the century club. Unlike the 1906 Cubs, the 1998 Yanks won the World Series. Through 1999, the century club included the 22 franchise names below. Find them in the word search. Look closely, because the names appear horizontally, vertically, diagonally and backwards.

(Answers are on page 121.)

```
C  A  R  D  I  N  A  L  S  L  Q  K  X  U  Q
O  H  S  K  L  V  R  S  E  V  A  R  B  X  U
E  G  L  Q  V  P  M  S  W  C  D  P  O  M  S
P  I  A  O  R  S  N  I  W  T  H  S  L  Z  O
P  A  Y  H  T  A  X  O  S  D  E  R  V  B  R
H  N  O  R  I  O  L  E  S  T  T  X  Y  Q  T
I  T  R  D  R  I  X  F  I  P  E  Z  O  S  S
L  S  N  N  E  A  T  H  L  E  T  I  C  S  A
L  I  S  T  E  M  W  S  A  B  R  E  P  U  S
I  S  K  C  A  B  D  N  O  M  A  I  D  Q  L
E  T  N  F  S  B  E  A  N  E  A  T  E  R  S
S  O  A  U  D  Q  Y  A  N  K  E  E  S  K  I
B  S  X  G  E  E  E  X  I  N  P  J  Q  Q  L
U  Z  G  E  R  Q  T  I  G  E  R  S  C  X  P
C  D  O  D  G  E  R  S  P  I  R  A  T  E  S
```

Search Words:

ASTROS

SUPERBAS

PIRATES

GIANTS

BRAVES

WHITE SOX

ROYALS

ORIOLES

DIAMONDBACKS

ATHLETICS

TIGERS

REDS

INDIANS

CARDINALS

YANKEES

PHILLIES

DODGERS

BEANEATERS

TWINS

RED SOX

METS

CUBS

DID YOU KNOW?

The Philadelphia Athletics head the century club for losers in the American League. The Athletics were 36–117 for the AL's record worst season, in 1916. The National League's Cleveland Spiders set the all-time Major League futility record of 20–134 in 1899.

8
MIDSUMMER TRADITIONS

Baseball throws two summertime parties. One is the All-Star Game, a movable feast that began in 1933 to showcase the fans' favorites in a glorified pick-up game between the American League and the National League. The other is the Hall of Fame induction weekend, a midsummer tradition since 1939 in Cooperstown, New York. It isn't as glitzy, but it's no less important on the baseball calendar because the induction ceremony salutes the greats of yesteryear while the Hall of Fame Game offers fans a preview of potential Hall of Famers.

(Answers are on page 94.)

8.1 **Who was the oldest pitcher in All-Star history?**
A. Nolan Ryan
B. Joe Niekro
C. Gaylord Perry
D. Satchel Paige

8.2 **Willie Mays and Hank Aaron are two of the three players who appeared in a record 24 All-Star Games. Who is the third?**
A. Mickey Mantle
B. Stan Musial
C. Brooks Robinson
D. Nolan Ryan

8.3 **Who has the record for most hits in All-Star play?**
A. Ty Cobb
B. Pete Rose
C. Willie Mays
D. Hank Aaron

8.4   Of the record ten All-Star Games that Casey Stengel managed, how many did he win?
A. Ten
B. Eight
C. Six
D. Four

8.5   Who was the first pitcher to win three All-Star Games?
A. Lefty Gomez
B. Roger Clemens
C. Nolan Ryan
D. Juan Marichal

8.6   In which inning did 1967's All-Star Game – the longest ever – end?
A. 12th inning
B. 15th inning
C. 16th inning
D. 20th inning

8.7   In what year was the All-Star Game played in August and before a record crowd?
A. 1933
B. 1959
C. 1981
D. 1995

8.8   Who was the first pitcher to strike out six batters in an All-Star Game?
A. Roger Clemens
B. Carl Hubbell
C. Ferguson Jenkins
D. Nolan Ryan

8.9 He was the American League rookie of the year and most valuable player in 1975. He hit a grand slam in 1983's All-Star Game. Who is he?

A. John Montefusco
B. George Brett
C. Jim Rice
D. Fred Lynn

8.10 Who was the first American League starting pitcher to win the All-Star Game in his home ballpark?

A. Pedro Martinez
B. Lefty Grove
C. Carl Hubbell
D. Lefty Gomez

8.11 How many players became Hall of Fame members in their first year of eligibility in 1999, the hall's 60th anniversary?

A. None
B. Two
C. Three
D. Seven

8.12 Who was the first player to hit safely four times in an All-Star Game?

A. Joe Medwick
B. Ted Williams
C. Arky Vaughn
D. Carl Yastrzemski

8.13 Which baseball great was late for the first Hall of Fame induction ceremony?

A. Babe Ruth
B. Cy Young
C. "Wee" Willie Keeler
D. Ty Cobb

8.14 Which pitcher with a colorful name led the American League to its only All-Star victory over the National League in a 20-year span?
A. Red Ruffing
B. Whitey Ford
C. Vida Blue
D. Mordecai Brown

8.15 Which American League team owner invited fans to literally break records before a game?
A. Tom Yawkey
B. Charles O. Finley
C. George Steinbrenner
D. Bill Veeck

8.16 What is the name of the site of the Hall of Fame Game?
A. Doubleday Field
B. Doubleday Park
C. Cooperstown Stadium
D. Otsego Diamond

8.17 Which Hall of Famer's baseball card is the most valuable?
A. Babe Ruth
B. Ty Cobb
C. Cy Young
D. Honus Wagner

8.18 Why did Ted Williams not play from 1943 to 1945?
A. Injury
B. War
C. Suspension
D. Contract holdout

8.19 What year would have been Pete Rose's first year of eligibility for election to the Hall of Fame?
A. 1989
B. 1991
C. 1992
D. 1999

MIDSUMMER TRADITIONS
Answers

8.1 **D. Satchel Paige**
At the age of 47 years and seven days, Satchel Paige was the oldest player in All-Star Game history when he pitched for the American League in Cincinnati on July 14, 1953. The National League won the game 5–1, and Paige saw action in the eighth inning. His only All-Star Game appearance was a disappointment because he yielded two runs on three singles and a walk. Paige, inducted into the Hall of Fame's Negro leagues section in 1971, came to the Indians when owner Bill Veeck purchased his contract from the Kansas City Monarchs in 1948. On the other end of the scale, the New York Mets' Dwight Gooden was the youngest player in an All-Star Game at the age of 19 years, seven months and 24 days in 1984. Gooden and the NL were 3–1 winners.

8.2 **B. Stan Musial**
Stan "The Man" Musial was among three players who played in 24 All-Star Games. Every season from 1943 to his retirement in 1963, the St. Louis Cardinals star played in the midsummer classic. Center fielder Willie Mays of the Giants and right fielder Hank Aaron of the Braves played with Musial for the National League. Mays's first All-Star Game was in 1954. He was in his 24th consecutive All-Star Game in 1973. Aaron played 23 times for the NL, beginning in 1955. He appeared once for the American League in 1975. Mays and Aaron share the record for playing 17 times on the winning club. Baltimore Orioles

third baseman Brooks Robinson, however, lost a record 15 times with the AL.

8.3 **C. Willie Mays**
Willie Mays is the all-time All-Star hitting champ. He hit 23 times in 75 at-bats and scored 20 runs for the National League. The 1979 Hall of Famer's three triples are a career record, shared with Brooks Robinson, who was inducted in 1983. Mays had eight extra base hits, the same number as NL teammate Stan Musial, a 1969 inductee. Musial also hit a record six home runs.

8.4 **D. Four**
New York Yankees manager Casey Stengel managed ten All-Star Games for the American League, but won only four times. His six losses are also a record. Of his ten All-Star appearances, a record five were consecutive, between 1950 and 1954. He had a better record in the World Series, leading his Yankees to seven titles in 12 seasons. For his efforts, he was inducted into the Hall of Fame in 1966. Walter Alston managed a record seven winning teams for the National League. Alston managed 23 years with the Brooklyn and Los Angeles Dodgers, beginning in 1954. He was inducted into the Hall of Fame in 1983. Under his guidance, the Dodgers won one World Series championship in Brooklyn and three in Los Angeles.

8.5 **A. Lefty Gomez**
New York Yankees left-handed pitcher Lefty Gomez was the first three-time winner in All-Star Game history. He won the July 6, 1933, inaugural match in Chicago's Comiskey Park 4–2 over the National League. He started, and won, again on July 8, 1935, in Cleveland's Municipal Stadium. His six-inning appearance in the 4–1 AL victory is the longest by a pitcher in All-Star history. Gomez's third win came at Griffith Stadium in Washington, D.C., on July 7, 1937, when the AL won 8–3. Gomez was inducted into the Hall of Fame in 1972.

PLAYERS SELECTED FOR
THE MOST ALL-STAR GAMES

Player	Games
Hank Aaron	25
Willie Mays	24
Stan Musial	24
Mickey Mantle	20
Ted Williams	19

8.6 **B. 15th inning**

A dozen pitchers combined to strike out 30 batters in the 15-inning All-Star Game on July 11, 1967, at Anaheim Stadium. Tony Perez hit a home run to give the National League a 2–1 victory. The three-hour and 41-minute game was the longest by innings and time. The NL's Ferguson Jenkins had a record-tying six strikeouts, while catcher Bill Freehan went the distance for the AL. The July 7, 1998, game at Coors Field in Denver, won 13–8 by the AL, was a nine-inning affair but three minutes shy of the record. The fastest All-Star Game lasted 1:53 in St. Louis on July 9, 1940. The NL won 4–0 on the strength of three first-inning runs and another in the eighth.

8.7 **C. 1981**

The August 9, 1981, All-Star Game at Cleveland's Municipal Stadium drew a record 72,086 fans. They saw Montreal Expos catcher Gary Carter hit two home runs for the most valuable player award and a 5–4 National League victory. It was the latest date on record for an All-Star Game. In fact, it was the first game played after a players' strike that lasted from June 12 to July 31. But it wasn't the only time the All-Star Game was played beyond July. On August 3, 1959, the AL won 5–3 at Los Angeles Memorial Coliseum in the first All-Star Game played on the west coast. The first All-Star Game that season resulted in a 5–4 NL win on July 7 in Pittsburgh. From 1959 to 1962, Major League baseball held two All-Star Games a year.

8.8   B. Carl Hubbell

The New York Giants' Carl Hubbell was the first to strike out six batters in an All-Star Game, on July 10, 1934, at the Polo Grounds in New York. Hubbell, a 1947 Hall of Famer, struck out five consecutive future Hall of Famers. They were (in order of appearance and disappearance): Babe Ruth, Lou Gehrig, Jimmie Foxx, Al Simmons and Joe Cronin in the first and second innings. As for walks, only one pitcher has issued five bases on balls in an All-Star Game: Bill Hallahan of the Chicago Cubs, on July 6, 1933.

8.9   D. Fred Lynn

Fred Lynn's third-inning grand slam for the American League in the July 6, 1983, All-Star Game at Comiskey Park in Chicago was his fourth All-Star home run and the first All-Star grand slam. Atlee Hammaker of the San Francisco Giants allowed the four-run homer and three other men to score, to claim the dubious honor of most runs allowed in an All-Star Game – seven. The AL coasted to a 13–3 win, and Lynn was named most valuable player as the 50th anniversary of the first All-Star Game was celebrated at the stadium where it all began.

8.10   A. Pedro Martinez

Boston Red Sox ace Pedro Martinez struck out the first three batters of the July 13, 1999, All-Star Game in Boston's Fenway Park, leading the American League to a 4–1 win over the National League. He was the first pitcher to strike out the first four batters of the game. Barry Larkin, Larry Walker and Sammy Sosa were Martinez's victims to begin the evening. He extended his streak to four batters by striking out Mark McGwire, the lead-off batter in the second inning. He also struck out Jeff Bagwell in the second inning to tie an American League record for most All-Star strikeouts and later became the first AL starter to win in his home park. Pitchers from both leagues also combined for an All-Star record 22 strikeouts (AL 12; NL 10).

HALL OF FAMERS BY
POSITION/CATEGORY, 1939–1999

Pitchers	58
Catchers	11
First basemen	16
Second basemen	14
Third basemen	9
Shortstops	19
Left fielders	18
Center fielders	16
Right fielders	21
Managers	15
Umpires	8
Pioneers/executives	23
Negro leaguers	16

8.11 **C. Three**

Nolan Ryan, George Brett and Robin Yount were the first three players voted to the Hall of Fame in the same year in their first year of eligibility since 1936. The election was announced on January 5, 1999. Three more inductees were named to the veterans' category and one in the Negro leagues' wing: 17-year first baseman Orlando Cepeda, AL umpire Nestor Chylak, manager Frank Selee and Joe Williams, a pitcher in the Negro leagues. The seven were inducted in the 60th anniversary ceremony at the Hall of Fame in Cooperstown on July 25, 1999.

8.12   A. Joe Medwick

Joe Medwick was the first player to hit four times safely in an All-Star Game. The St. Louis Cardinals' left fielder, elected to the Hall of Fame in 1968, did it in 1937. The Boston Red Sox's Ted Williams and Carl Yastrzemski, both Hall of Famers, repeated the feat in 1946 and 1970, respectively. In the 1946 game, Williams set the record for most RBIs (five) and runs scored (four), thanks to his pair of home runs.

8.13   D. Ty Cobb

Ty Cobb nearly missed the first Hall of Fame induction ceremony in Cooperstown on June 12, 1939. Cobb's arrival was delayed because he traveled to the event from California, though some speculate that his tardiness was meant to upstage his foe, Kenesaw Mountain Landis, a judge who was baseball's first commissioner. Landis was there to preside over the ceremony and open the Hall of Fame. The other ten living Hall of Famers were already there and posed for a group photo: Connie Mack, Honus Wagner, Walter Johnson, Babe Ruth, Nap Lajoie, Tris Speaker, Cy Young, Grover Cleveland Alexander, George Sisler and Eddie Collins. ("Wee" Willie Keeler and Christy Mathewson were inducted posthumously.) It wasn't a national holiday, but all 16 Major League ballparks were closed to observe the occasion.

8.14   C. Vida Blue

The National League won 19 of 20 All Star Games from 1963 to 1982 (including 11 consecutive). The only loss during the dynasty came when All-Star rookie starter Vida Blue of the Oakland Athletics pitched the American League to a 6–4 victory on July 13, 1971, at Detroit's Tiger Stadium. The AL hadn't won since 1962 and wouldn't beat the NL again until 1983.

8.15   D. Bill Veeck

Fans who brought a disco record to Comiskey Park on July 12, 1979, could buy tickets to the Chicago White Sox doubleheader against the Detroit Tigers for 98 cents in a promotion sponsored by 98 WLUP, a Chicago FM radio station. Disco Demolition Night was another of White Sox owner Bill Veeck's colorful promotions – except this one went horribly wrong and cost his team at least one win. Some fans threw their records on the field during play in the first game, won 4–1 by the Tigers. Between games, the records were gathered and blown to pieces by dynamite in center field. But the explosion touched off a near-riot when thousands of fans jumped the fences. Seventy-six minutes later, chief umpire Dave Phillips postponed the game because sod was missing and shards of vinyl were scattered around the field. A day later, American League president Lee MacPhail Jr. awarded Detroit a 9–0 win. (It is not known whether the Tigers' players went disco dancing to celebrate.) Veeck, who once owned the Cleveland Indians and St. Louis Browns, was inducted into the Hall of Fame in 1991. He was known for his stunts, such as hiring three-foot-seven Eddie Gaedel to play for the Browns in 1951 and for giving away guinea pigs. On a more serious note, he helped break baseball's color barrier in 1947 when he signed Larry Doby, the AL's first black American player, to the Indians.

PITCHERS SELECTED FOR MOST ALL-STAR GAMES

Pitcher	Games
Warren Spahn	17
Tom Seaver	12
Steve Carlton	10
Whitey Ford	10
Juan Marichal	10

8.16 **A. Doubleday Field**

In a six-inning game at Doubleday Field on June 12, 1939, a team managed by career National Leaguer Honus Wagner beat a side led by American League mainstay Eddie Collins 4–2. It was baseball's first "Hall of Fame Game," an event that would annually coincide with the induction ceremonies at the nearby Hall of Fame. Beginning in 1940, the exhibition game featured franchises from the American and National leagues. Doubleday Field, which seats 9,791, opened in 1920 in a former cow pasture that was the mythical site of the first baseball game in 1839: it was said to involve Abner Doubleday and local schoolboys.

8.17 D. Honus Wagner

Honus Wagner, "the Flying Dutchman," played in the National League for 21 years and performed so well at the plate and in the field that some consider him the game's best all-around player. He began his career with the Louisville Colonels in 1897, but his finest years were in a Pittsburgh Pirates uniform. He batted better than .300 for 15 consecutive seasons, had 3,415 hits and stole 722 bases during his career. He was among the first class of Hall of Famers elected in 1936. In 1910, a portrait of Wagner appeared on a baseball card in a set distributed with packages of American Tobacco Company cigarettes. Wagner, who wasn't paid, insisted that his card be discontinued because he disliked cigarettes. By the 1990s, as few as 25 of the cards were said to remain. Hockey superstar Wayne Gretzky and Los Angeles Kings owner Bruce McNall bought one for $451,000 at an auction in 1991. The same card sold five years later for $650,000. Collector Barry Halper donated the Wagner card on display at the Hall of Fame in 1984.

8.18 B. War

Ted Williams – nicknamed "the Splendid Splinter" – served in the U.S. military as a World War II bomber pilot over the Pacific from 1943 to 1945. He also flew in the Korean War and missed most of the 1952 and 1953 seasons. Pitchers Bob Feller and Warren Spahn were other Hall of Famers who fought in World War II. Williams, a San Diego native, spent his entire 19-year career with the Boston Red Sox and batted under .300 only once. He retired in 1960 and hit a home run in his last at-bat,

September 26, 1960, on a 1–1 pitch from Baltimore Orioles hurler Jack Fisher into the right-field bleachers. Williams' 521st home run gave the Red Sox a 5–4 win. Despite a standing ovation and cheers of "we want Ted" from the Fenway Park crowd, Williams did not emerge from the dugout to offer a tip of the cap. He was elected to the Hall of Fame in 1966 but returned to baseball as a manager. From 1969 to 1971, he managed the Washington Senators and moved with them to Texas when they became the Rangers in 1972. As a player he never batted .429, but he registered a disappointing .429 winning percentage as the dugout boss in Washington, D.C., and Arlington, Texas, with a 273–364 record. He was honored in a pre-game ceremony at the 1999 All-Star Game in Boston as part of celebrations to commemorate baseball's best players of the twentieth century.

DID YOU KNOW?

Nine of the first 70 All-Star Games went to extra innings, and all nine were won by the National League. The first time this happened was on July 11, 1950, at Chicago's Comiskey Park, where Pittsburgh Pirate Ralph Kiner tied the game in the top of the ninth inning with a home run. St. Louis Cardinals second baseman Red Schoendienst took advantage of the opening pitch by Detroit Tiger Ted Gray and homered in the 14th inning. The 4–3 win was also the first for the NL as the visiting team.

Tony Perez, who was named to the Hall of Fame in 2000, ended the longest game in All-Star history on July 11, 1967, in the 15th inning: the Cincinnati Reds' third baseman hit a home run off Kansas City Athletics pitcher Jim "Catfish" Hunter for the 2–1 NL win at Anaheim Stadium.

Four other NL wins came in the 10th inning, another two were in the 12th and one was in the 13th.

8.19 C. 1992

Pete Rose had five hits, including the 4,256th of his career, on August 11, 1986, for the Cincinnati Reds. It was 45-year-old Rose's last appearance as a player, but he continued as the Reds' manager until his forced retirement in 1989. Players must be retired for five calendar years to be eligible for inclusion in Hall of Fame balloting. So Rose's first year of eligibility for induction would have been 1992, when he received 41 write-in votes from members of the Baseball Writers' Association of America. Rose's name was prohibited from the ballot because he was banned from baseball by then-commissioner A. Bartlett Giamatti on August 24, 1989, for gambling on baseball games. Anticipating Rose's imminent candidacy, a special committee of the Hall of Fame decided that players like Rose who were ineligible to participate in Major League baseball were also ineligible to become members of the Hall of Fame.

Game Eight

HALL OF FAME CROSSWORD

You don't have to be a record-setter to become a member of baseball's Hall of Fame, but it certainly helps. Test your Hall of Fame knowledge with this crossword.

(*Answers are on page 121.*)

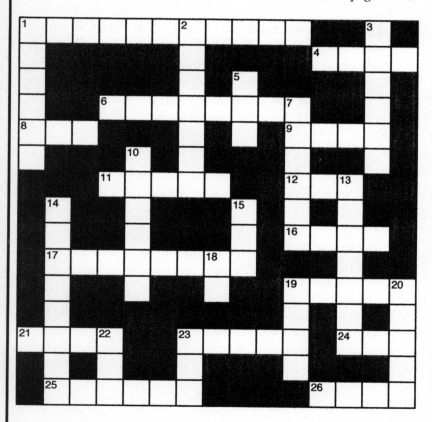

Across

1 Hall of Fame is in this village (11 letters)

4 _____ Marichal pitched in eight All-Star Games (4)

6 First commissioner Kenesaw _____ Landis (8)

8 _____ Drysdale pitched 58 ⅔ shutout innings in a row in 1968 (3)

9 _____ Averill was first American Leaguer to homer in first at-bat (4)

11 Doubleday _____ , site of Hall of Fame Game (5)

12 _____ Brock, World Series stolen-base leader (3)

16 _____ Rixey, winningest left-hander before Warren Spahn (4)

17 Brooks, Frank, Wilbert and Jackie's last name (8)

19 _____ baseman Lou Gehrig (5)

21 Ty _____ (4)

23 Brothers Paul and Lloyd _____ (5)

24 Babe Ruth's first team, the Boston Red _____ (3)

25 Joe DiMaggio, the "_____ Clipper" (6)

26 Tom Seaver of the New York _____ recorded ten consecutive strikeouts in 1970 (4)

Down

1 Pitcher Ferguson Jenkins, the first Hall of Famer from _____ (6 letters)

2 Manager Casey _____ managed a record five World Series winners in a row (7)

3 Mickey _____ hit a record 18 World Series home runs (6)

5 Stan "The _____ " Musial played in 24 All-Star Games (3)

7 _____ Fox played a record 798 consecutive games at second base (6)

10 "Say hey" _____ Mays (6)

13 Bill Klem and Tom Connolly, the first Hall of Fame _____ (7)

14 Induction _____ (8)

15 _____ Diego, birthplace of Ted Williams (3)

18 Sadaharu _____ hit 868 home runs in Japan, but is not yet a Hall of Fame member (2)

19 Whitey _____ has the most wins and strikeouts in World Series history (4)

20 All-time strikeout leader Nolan Ryan's home state (5)

22 American League founder _____ Johnson (3)

23 "_____" Willie Keeler (3)

9

AUTUMN MAGIC

The days grow shorter, temperatures become cooler, the leaves on trees change colors and fall to the ground. And baseball playoffs begin for the handful of teams that reaped the most wins in the six-month regular season. Only one team will take home the World Series trophy. But the most unlikely of players on winning or losing sides are capable of rising to the occasion and performing spectacular feats in October. Here's your chance to go out on top.

(*Answers are on page 110.*)

9.1 **Who was the first player to record seven runs batted in during a post-season game?**
A. Mo Vaughn
B. Babe Ruth
C. Edgar Martinez
D. Troy O'Leary

9.2 **What 1920 World Series team was Bill Wambsganss on when he turned the only unassisted triple play in post-season history?**
A. Cleveland Indians
B. Brooklyn Robins
C. Philadelphia Athletics
D. Boston Red Sox

9.3 **What year witnessed the first home run by a pitcher and first grand slam home run in World Series history?**
A. 1903
B. 1920
C. 1961
D. 1998

9.4   What is the record for the most strikeouts in a World Series game?
   A. 15
   B. 17
   C. 19
   D. 21

9.5   How old was Jack Quinn when he became the oldest pitcher to finish a World Series game?
   A. 40
   B. 44
   C. 45
   D. 46

9.6   How many games did it take Lou Brock to tie the World Series record for most career stolen bases?
   A. 14
   B. 21
   C. 26
   D. 34

9.7   Who pitched the most innings in a single World Series game and was the first to have home runs in consecutive innings of a World Series game?
   A. Babe Ruth
   B. Bob Lemon
   C. Walter Johnson
   D. Christy Mathewson

9.8   What New York Yankees slugger was dubbed "Mr. October" and hit a record five home runs in a World Series?
   A. Mickey Mantle
   B. Babe Ruth
   C. Steve Garvey
   D. Reggie Jackson

9.9 John Wetteland was the most valuable player of the 1996 World Series. What role did he play?
A. Designated hitter
B. Relief pitcher
C. Starting pitcher
D. Pinch-hitter

9.10 Robin Ventura was the last batter in the longest game in post-season history, on October 17, 1999. How did he score the game-winning run to end the marathon?
A. Grand slam home run
B. Two-run home run
C. Bases-loaded walk
D. Single

9.11 What team set records for most runs and hits in a 1999 post-season game?
A. Boston Red Sox
B. Cleveland Indians
C. New York Yankees
D. Atlanta Braves

9.12 Who pitched the most World Series games and innings and recorded the most wins and losses in the fall classic?
A. Bob Gibson
B. Whitey Ford
C. Babe Ruth
D. Bob Feller

9.13 Where was the first World Series–ending home run hit?
A. Yankee Stadium, New York
B. Ebbets Field, Brooklyn
C. Wrigley Field, Chicago
D. Forbes Field, Pittsburgh

9.14 When did the New York Yankees win the first of their record five consecutive World Series championships?
A. 1936
B. 1947
C. 1949
D. 1996

9.15 How many World Series rings did Yogi Berra earn?
A. Five
B. Six
C. Ten
D. 14

9.16 How did Patsy Dougherty score in the bottom of the first inning of the second-ever World Series game between American League and National League teams?
A. Grand slam home run
B. Stole home
C. Inside-the-park home run
D. Walked home

9.17 What is the record for hitting the most batsmen in a World Series game?
A. Two
B. Three
C. Four
D. Five

9.18 Which World Series had the highest attendance?
A. Los Angeles Dodgers vs. Chicago White Sox, 1959
B. Chicago White Sox vs. Chicago Cubs, 1906
C. Florida Marlins vs. Cleveland Indians, 1997
D. New York Yankees vs. Atlanta Braves, 1999

9.19 When did Bernie Carbo record two pinch-hit home runs in one World Series?
A. 1947
B. 1955
C. 1975
D. 1988

9.20 Why was the 1994 World Series canceled?
A. Earthquake
B. War
C. Strike
D. Flu outbreak

AUTUMN MAGIC
Answers

9.1 C. Edgar Martinez

New York native Edgar Martinez was the first to record seven RBIs in a post-season game. He led his Seattle Mariners to an 11–8 home victory on October 7, 1995, over the New York Yankees in game four of an American League Division Series. The Yankees led 5–0 until Martinez hit a three-run homer in the third inning. In the eighth inning, he hit a tie-breaking grand slam. Martinez continued to be the hero in the series' fifth and deciding game the next day. His two-run double in the 11th inning gave Seattle a 6–5 win. Three Boston Red Sox players tied Martinez's record in games against the Cleveland Indians during the 1998 and 1999 playoffs. Mo Vaughn had a three-run homer, two-run homer and two-run double on September 29, 1998, for the Red Sox in an 11–3 win at Cleveland in game one of the ALDS. John Valentin and Troy O'Leary repeated the feat in successive games a year later, on October 10 and 11, in the ALDS at Fenway Park. Valentin's seven RBIs came in a 23–7 game four win. O'Leary had his seven in the series-clinching 11–8 game five win. His grand slam was the first for the Red Sox in post-season play.

9.2 **A. Cleveland Indians**

Second baseman Bill Wambsganss, a native of Cleveland, made history in game five of the 1920 World Series for his Indians. Wambsganss turned the first and only unassisted triple play in post-season history on October 10, 1920, against the Brooklyn Robins. The Robins trailed 7–0 and put two men on base in the fifth inning. Pitcher Clarence Mitchell hit a line drive to Wambsganss, who got Pete Kilduff out at second and tagged Otto Miller on the baseline to end the inning. Cleveland won the game 8–1 and went on to take the series 5–2.

9.3 **B. 1920**

October 10, 1920, was a day of many firsts. While Bill Wambsganss turned the first unassisted triple play in World Series history, his Cleveland Indians teammates Elmer Smith and Jim Bagby made offensive feats. Smith hit the first grand slam in World Series history with a blast in the first inning off Brooklyn Robins pitcher Burleigh Grimes at Municipal Stadium in Cleveland. Bagby, who led the majors with 31 regular-season wins, was the starting pitcher for the Indians and went the distance for the 8–1 victory. Bagby's three-run homer in the third inning was the first home run by a pitcher in a World Series.

9.4 **B. 17**

Bob Gibson of the St. Louis Cardinals struck out a record 17 Detroit Tigers in game one of the World Series on October 2, 1968. The five-hit shutout was good enough for a 4–0 victory. Gibson pitched two more complete games and struck out 18 more for the World Series record of 35. The Tigers, however, went seven games to win the series. Baltimore Oriole Moe Drabowsky allowed one hit and struck out 11 Los Angeles Dodgers in a 6⅔-inning relief assignment on October 5, 1966, in game one of the World Series – the most strikeouts by a relief pitcher in a World Series game. Drabowsky got the win, and the Orioles swept the Dodgers in four games. The one-inning record for most strikeouts belongs to Orval Overall of the Chicago

Cubs. He fanned four Detroit Tigers to begin game five of the World Series on October 14, 1908. (One of the batters reached first base on a wild pitch.) Overall pitched a complete game victory, his second of the series, to give the Cubs a 2–0 win and the championship.

9.5   D. 46

Jack Quinn of the Philadelphia Athletics was the oldest pitcher to start and finish a World Series game. On October 4, 1930, Quinn was the last of three Athletics pitchers in game three of the World Series, a 5–0 win against the St. Louis Cardinals. Quinn, then 46 years, two months and 29 days old, pitched two innings. Grover Cleveland Alexander was the oldest pitcher to go the distance, when his St. Louis Cardinals defeated the New York Yankees 10–2 on October 9, 1926. He was 39 years, seven months and 13 days old. The youngest pitcher to win a game in the World Series was Joe Bush. His Athletics beat the New York Giants 8–2 in game three on October 9, 1913. Bush was 20 years, 10 months and 12 days old.

9.6   B. 21

Stop that man! It took Lou Brock 21 games to steal 14 bases and tie Eddie Collins's World Series record for most stolen bases. Collins stole ten for the Philadelphia Athletics and four for the Chicago White Sox over 34 games in six World Series. Brock played 21 games in three World Series. He failed to steal a base during his first trip to the fall classic in 1964, but he had seven in both 1967 and 1968. The totals are both records for single World Series. Brock also became the first to tie the World Series record for most stolen bases in a single game twice. Honus Wagner of the Pittsburgh Pirates was the first player to steal three in a World Series game, on October 11, 1909.

9.7   A. Babe Ruth

Babe Ruth was the first player to hit home runs in consecutive innings of a World Series game. He did it on October 11, 1923, in the fourth and fifth innings of the New York Yankees' 4–2 win over the New York Giants in game two. He did it again almost five years later, on October 9, 1928, when he homered in innings seven and eight of the 7–3 game four win over the St. Louis Cardinals to complete a four-game sweep. Before Ruth terrorized pitchers, he was a pitcher. In the 1916 World Series, Ruth pitched a record 14 innings with the Boston Red Sox on October 9, 1916, in a 2–1 game two defeat of the Brooklyn Robins; teams didn't have the luxury of fully staffed bullpens in those days. The Red Sox eventually won the series, 4–1.

9.8   D. Reggie Jackson

New York Yankees catcher Thurman Munson called outfielder Reggie Jackson "Mr. October" early in the 1977 World Series. It's a name Jackson quickly earned when he hit a record five home runs in three games against the Los Angeles Dodgers. Jackson homered in games four and five and then hit three homers on a record three consecutive pitches in game six, on October 18. The 8–4 win gave the Yankees their first World Series championship since 1962. Jackson hit two-run homers off Burt Hooton and Elias Sosa in the fourth and fifth innings, respectively. His third of the game – and record fifth of the series – was an eighth-inning solo shot off Charlie Hough.

9.9   B. Relief pitcher

It was quality, not quantity for John Wetteland of the New York Yankees. He appeared in only 4⅓ innings over five games as a relief pitcher in the 1996 World Series against the Atlanta Braves. But that was enough to snag the most valuable player award. Wetteland had a World Series–record four saves. He limited the Braves to four hits, one run and one walk and struck out six. His fourth save came on October 26, 1996, when the Yankees clinched the championship in the sixth game with a 3–2 win. Wetteland led the American League with 43 regular-season saves and finished the playoffs with an additional seven.

9.10 D. Single

Robin Ventura came to the plate with the bases loaded in the bottom of the 15th inning for the New York Mets in the 1999 National League Championship Series' fifth game on October 17. He hit what appeared to be a grand slam home run over the right-field fence at Shea Stadium. But Ventura's teammates mobbed him at second base. He never made it to home plate, so the winning RBI of the five-hour and 46-minute game was scored officially as a single and the final score was 4–3.

BATTERS WHO HIT FOUR OR MORE HOME RUNS IN A SINGLE WORLD SERIES

Player	Team	HRs	Year	Games
Babe Ruth	New York Yankees	4	1926	7
Lou Gehrig	New York Yankees	4	1928	4
Duke Snider	Brooklyn Dodgers	4	1952	7
Duke Snider	Brooklyn Dodgers	4	1955	7
Hank Bauer	New York Yankees	4	1958	7
Gene Tenace	Oakland Athletics	4	1972	7
Reggie Jackson	New York Yankees	5	1977	6
Willie Aikens	Kansas City Royals	4	1980	6
Lenny Dykstra	Philadelphia Phillies	4	1993	6

9.11 A. Boston Red Sox

Records fell like autumn leaves on October 10, 1999, in game four of an American League Division Series at Boston's Fenway Park. The Boston Red Sox beat the Cleveland Indians 23–7, setting post-season records for runs and hits. The 23 runs surpassed the New York Yankees' 18-run World Series record against the New York Giants on October 2, 1936. The 24 hits were two more than the Atlanta Braves' October 14, 1996, total of 22 in a 14–0 win over the St. Louis Cardinals in game five of the

National League Championship Series. The Red Sox and Indians' combined 30 runs was one better than the 29 scored when the Toronto Blue Jays edged the Philadelphia Phillies 15–14 in game four of the World Series on October 20, 1993. To top it all off, the Red Sox scored more runs than 19 National Football League teams had points on that Sunday.

9.12   B. Whitey Ford

Whitey Ford got his first World Series victory in the first World Series game he started. The New York–born left-hander led the Yankees to a 5–2 win over the Philadelphia Phillies to cap a four-game World Series sweep on October 7, 1950. The rookie struck out seven Phillies and took the Yankees into the ninth inning with a shutout. Ford, nicknamed the "Chairman of the Board," went on to set a plethora of World Series pitching records. He started in 22 World Series games over 11 championships until 1964. He struck out 94 and walked 34 in 146 innings pitched. He even recorded 33 consecutive scoreless innings from 1960 to 1962.

9.13   D. Forbes Field

Bill Mazeroski broke a 9–9 tie in the ninth inning of the seventh and deciding game of the 1960 World Series on October 13. He launched New York Yankees pitcher Ralph Terry's second pitch of the inning over the left-field wall to give the Pittsburgh Pirates a 10–9 win and their first World Series championship since 1925. Mazeroski's second four-bagger of the series was the first time a World Series ended with a home run. It also completed a dramatic upset of the heavily favored Yankees, who outscored Pittsburgh 55–27. The 82 runs by both teams set a record for a post-season series. The Yankees were also the highest-scoring World Series loser in history. Thirty-three years later at Toronto's SkyDome, Joe Carter lifted his Blue Jays over the Philadelphia Phillies to win their second consecutive World Series, on October 23, 1993. Carter's two-run homer off reliever Mitch Williams over the left-field fence gave the Blue Jays an 8–6 victory. It was only the second World Series-ending homer. For

Blue Jays fans, it was even more special: it was the first time a World Series ended outside the United States and with a Canadian team as champion.

DID YOU KNOW?

On December 12, 1998, the Los Angeles Dodgers signed 33-year-old pitcher Kevin Brown to a seven-year, $105 million deal – the biggest pitching contract in baseball history. Brown had helped the San Diego Padres win the 1998 National League pennant. Seventy-seven years earlier, Babe Ruth was paid a then-record $50,000 to play for the 1922 New York Yankees.

9.14 C. 1949

The New York Yankees, under manager Casey Stengel, won five consecutive World Series beginning in 1949. Only once during the string of championships did the Yankees have to go the full seven games. That was in 1952, against the Brooklyn Dodgers. The Cleveland Indians put an end to the streak in 1954, when they finished first in the American League with 111 regular-season wins – a record that stood until the Yankees won 114 in 1998. The Indians lost the World Series in four straight games to the New York Giants, thus keeping the championship in the Big Apple for the sixth consecutive year. The five straight wins beat the Yankees' own record of four in a row, between 1936 and 1939.

9.15 C. Ten

New York Yankees great Yogi Berra was a member of a record ten World Series–winning Yankees teams during his career. He hit a career record 71 hits for the Yankees in 75 games over 14 series. He's also the only catcher to call a World Series perfect game: he was behind the plate for pitcher Don Larsen's perfect World Series game on October 8, 1956. He also managed the Yankees in 1964 and 1984–85 but was fired by owner George Steinbrenner during the second tour of duty. That caused Berra to boycott Yankee Stadium for almost 14 years. Steinbrenner apologized in early 1999 and welcomed him back for Yogi Berra Day on July 18. That was the day Larsen threw the ceremonial first pitch to Berra, who borrowed catcher Joe Girardi's mitt for the occasion. Then starter David Cone pitched the third perfect game in Yankee Stadium history, over the Montreal Expos.

MOST WORLD SERIES CHAMPIONSHIPS, BY FRANCHISE (1903–1999)

Team	Wins	
New York Yankees	25	
St. Louis Cardinals	9	
Athletics	9	(5 in Philadelphia, 4 in Oakland)
Dodgers	6	(5 in Los Angeles, 1 in Brooklyn)
New York Giants, Pittsburgh Pirates, Cincinnati Reds, Boston Red Sox	5	
Detroit Tigers	4	
Braves	3	(1 in Boston, 1 in Milwaukee, 1 in Atlanta)
Baltimore Orioles	3	

9.16   C. Inside-the-park home run

Boston Pilgrims outfielder Patsy Dougherty had the second home run in World Series history, on October 2, 1903. Dougherty led off the bottom of the first inning of game two against the Pittsburgh Pirates with an inside-the-park home run charged to pitcher Sam Leever. It was the first of ten World Series inside-the-park home runs in the 1900s.

9.17   B. Three

Maybe it was the bright lights that distracted Bruce Kison and caused him to hit three batters and set a World Series record on

October 13, 1971, during the first scheduled World Series game to be played at night. Regardless, the Pittsburgh Pirates' relief pitcher managed to give his team a 4–3 game four win over the Baltimore Orioles with 6 ⅓ innings pitched. The Pirates won the series in seven games. In 1907, Bill Donovan became the first pitcher to hit three batters in a World Series when he pitched for the Detroit Tigers in a loss to the Chicago Cubs. Donovan's first World Series start was game one on October 8, 1907, but the game ended in a 3–3, 12-inning tie because of darkness. It was the first of only three ties in World Series history.

9.18   **A.   Los Angeles Dodgers vs. Chicago White Sox, 1959**
The World Series came to the west coast for the first time in 1959, when the Chicago White Sox visited the Los Angeles Dodgers for games three, four and five. Game five, on October 6, drew 92,706 fans – the largest crowd to see a regular-season or playoff game. A total attendance of 420,784 was recorded for the six-game series. The Dodgers, who had won the World Series once in Brooklyn, moved from cozy Ebbets Field to the spacious Los Angeles Memorial Coliseum in 1958 after Dodgers owner Walter O'Malley's proposal to build a new domed stadium in New York was rejected.

9.19   **C.   1975**
Bernie Carbo of the Boston Red Sox was the first to hit two pinch-hit home runs in a World Series in 1975's classic against the Cincinnati Reds. On October 21, Carbo had his second homer of the series as a pinch-hitter in the eighth inning of game six with two men on base. The Red Sox won the game 7–6 on a dramatic home run by 2000 Hall of Famer Carlton Fisk in the 12th inning, but lost the series in seven games. Yogi Berra became the first to hit a pinch-hit home run in World Series history on October 2, 1947, in a 9–8 game three loss to the Brooklyn Dodgers.

C. Strike

The World Series was played during two world wars, and not even the 1989 San Francisco earthquake could stop it. But it was canceled in its second year, in 1904, when the New York Giants refused to play the Boston Pilgrims, who won the inaugural series between the champions of the American League and National League. Giants owner John Brush was satisfied with his team's NL pennant in 1904 and wasn't willing to risk it against a team from the lesser AL. The Giants beat the Philadelphia Athletics when the World Series resumed in 1905. On August 12, 1994, Major League baseball players went on strike because owners wanted to impose a salary cap. The remainder of the season and the World Series were canceled on September 14. On March 31, 1995, the National Labor Relations Board ruled against the owners, citing unfair bargaining practices. Players voted to return to their teams and play under the rules of the expired collective-bargaining agreement. The 234-day strike was the longest in sports history. In 1995, each team played 144 games – 18 fewer than normal.

DID YOU KNOW?

When the 1994 World Series was canceled by a strike, baseball fans eager to follow professional baseball had few options but to keep an eye on triple A playoffs. The last game of the year, on September 17, was the fifth and deciding game in the Pacific Coast League championship at Nat Bailey Stadium in Vancouver, British Columbia. The host Vancouver Canadians, the California Angels' top farm team, were edged by the Los Angeles Dodgers–affiliated Albuquerque Dukes 3–2 before 6,240 fans. The PCL crown was Dukes manager Rick Dempsey's first triple A championship and completed a rare feat: Dempsey already had titles in Little League, Pony, single A, double A and Major League baseball. Dempsey was the 1983 World Series' most valuable player with the champion Baltimore Orioles.

GAME ANSWERS

Game One: Record Numbers
1. L	4. A	7. E	9. K	11. I
2. J	5. D	8. B	10. F	12. C
3. G	6. H			

Game Two: Award-Winning Rookies
1. O	4. N	7. F	10. B	13. I
2. L	5. K	8. H	11. G	14. M
3. E	6. C	9. D	12. J	15. A

Game Three: Esteemed Yankees Name Scramble
ARRBE	Yogi BERR**A**	TURH	Babe **R**UTH
DORF	Whitey **F**ORD	SNOCKAJ	Reggie JACK**S**ON
THUNER	Catfish HUNT**E**R	ZZORITU	Phil RIZZUT**O**
HERGIG	Lou GE**H**RIG	GELNETS	Casey STENGE**L**
GOMAGIDI	Joe DI**MA**GGIO	FUFGRIN	Red RU**F**FING
NETLMA	Mickey MANT**LE**		

Put highlighted letters in correct order to spell: HALL OF FAMERS

Game Four: The Nickname Game
1. L. George "Sparky" Anderson	9. M. Edwin "Duke" Snider
2. E. Lawrence "Yogi" Berra	10. G. Charles "Casey" Stengel
3. D. Ed "Whitey" Ford	11. F. John "Honus" Wagner
4. C. Bob "Hoot" Gibson	12. N. Lloyd "Little Poison" Waner
5. B. Mark "Big Mac" McGwire	13. O. Paul "Big Poison" Waner
6. H. George "Highpockets" Kelly	14. A. Lewis "Hack" Wilson
7. J. Leroy "Satchel" Paige	15. I. Denton "Cy" Young
8. K. Pete "Charlie Hustle" Rose	

Game Five: They Said It
1. C	4. N	7. K	10. M	13. E
2. F	5. J	8. G	11. O	14. L
3. I	6. H	9. B	12. A	15. D

Game Six: Wonder Years
1. D	4. O	7. E	10. F	13. L
2. G	5. C	8. I	11. M	14. K
3. A	6. H	9. N	12. J	15. B

Game Seven: The Century Club Word Search

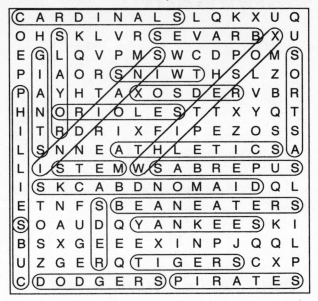

Game Eight: Hall of Fame Crossword

ACKNOWLEDGEMENTS

The author gratefully acknowledges the help of Eric Enders, William Francis and James Gates at the National Baseball Hall of Fame Library; Jeff Idelson of the National Baseball Hall of Fame and Museum; Rob Sanders, Terri Wershler, John Eerkes, Peter Cocking, Leanne Denis and the rest of the staff at Greystone Books; Jonathan, Jessica, Sherry and Robert Mackin, Sr.; Mick Maloney, Neville Judd, Martin Dunphy, Lloyd Gell, Joots Mistry, Robert Elliott, Christine Cosby, Sue and Barry Fast, Jim Bennie, Jay Berman, and Ray Crosato. A special thank-you to Henry Chadwick (1824–1908), baseball's first scorekeeper, statistician and journalist.

ABOUT THE AUTHOR

Bob Mackin is a sports writer with additional expertise in coverage of business, politics and music – both popular and unpopular. The native of Vernon, British Columbia, has called Vancouver's North Shore home for much of his life. During his teens and early twenties he was a press box assistant and substitute public-address announcer at Nat Bailey Stadium during Vancouver Canadians games. For four seasons he reported on Pacific Coast League baseball for the Canadian Press wire service and out-of-town daily newspapers. Bob, who still laments the loss of the C's to Sacramento, has worked as a sports editor with various suburban newspapers in Vancouver and writes a weekly sports column for the *Vancouver Courier*.